# Praise for *The*

"It turns out the long-hidden story of jack trice
is vivid, evocative, and inspiring."
—Bob Costas

"*The Idealist* is the historical account of Jack Trice—a Black man who grew up in the Cleveland area and went to Iowa State University as the school's first Black football player. It is a story that teaches us about the past and how much the past is in the present. I have more in common with this story than spending time in Cleveland and finding my escape through football. I too have felt the same responsibility to race, family, and self and can relate to this story, and I am confident that I am not alone. Our battles continue, but my prayer is that they will soon be won and the 'race war' will become something of the past. Thank you, Jonathan, for reminding us that the past is sometimes more important than the present, because without it, we would lose our way."
—Hue Jackson, former Oakland Raiders and Cleveland Browns head coach

"The Jack Trice story is one that every college football fan should know. It is a shame that Jack is not ingrained in our collective consciousness in the same way Rudy Ruettiger has been for overcoming personal obstacles to achieve his football dreams. Trice, a trailblazer in our sport, not only carried the weight of his own expectations but also those of his entire race. Jonathan Gelber shines a light on Jack Trice's rich family history, his purposeful life, his tragic death, and his enduring legacy."
—Desmond Howard, 1991 Heisman Trophy winner

"Cleveland East Technical High School has many proud graduates, but none are more impactful than Jesse Owens and Jack Trice. Now Jonathan Gelber's book will make Jack Trice's story known and understood by our nation."
—Jim Tressel, former college head coach who won a national championship with the Ohio State Buckeyes in 2002

"I admire and applaud Iowa State University for doing the right thing. Well-done, Iowa State, and well written, Dr. Gelber!"
—Steve Spurrier, former college football and NFL head coach who won a a national championship with the Florida Gators in 1996

"Being from Iowa, and having played quarterback at Iowa State, I know firsthand how important Jack Trice is to every Cyclone who walks on the Ames campus. You wouldn't expect the only major college football stadium named after an African American to be located in Ames, Iowa, but that's because you don't know the story of Jack Trice. His legacy as a Cyclone has made Iowa State a more inclusive institution, and his story has inspired thousands of ISU student-athletes to understand the value of sacrifice for their teams and families. The Jack Trice story represents everything that is good in the world of college athletics."

—Sage Rosenfels, Iowa State University quarterback
and veteran NFL quarterback

"This story is as important as ever. We have come a long way but not far enough. Stories like Jack's matter."

—Don Nelson, second-winningest coach in NBA history

"Jack Trice's legacy was an important part of my experience as a student-athlete at Iowa State University. His story and his character displayed traits such as grit, courage, and toughness. He dedicated his life to being his best self and ultimately gave his all."

—Kyven Gadson, three-time All-American wrestler, 2015
NCAA Division I champion, Iowa State University

"The little-known story of how Iowa State University, after many years, finally came to name its football stadium after 'some poor dead Black kid'—Jack Trice—is a terrific saga that brilliantly intertwines race, sports, and a special slice of African American history. Jonathan Gelber's research for this book appears impeccable, fueling an insightful biography of Trice—whose career at Iowa State lasted only two games. But this book also offers an intriguing look at how Black history overlapped with sports history during an era when Black athletes were anomalies in White collegiate programs. Trice's story is a tragic one, but his endearing impact, spirit, and historic status as one of the school's first Black students moved ISU students—of *all* races—to fight and persevere to provide the Trice legacy a well-deserved honor. It's a story that needs to be told."

—Michael Hurd, author of *Thursday Night Lights* and *Black College Football 1892–1992: One Hundred Years of History, Education, and Pride*

# THE IDEALIST

# THE IDEALIST

Jack Trice and the Battle for a
Forgotten Football Legacy

Jonathan Gelber M.D., M.S.

TRIUMPH
BOOKS

This book is available in quantity at special discounts for your group or organization. For further information, contact:
   **Triumph Books LLC**
   814 North Franklin Street
   Chicago, Illinois 60610
   (312) 337-0747
   www.triumphbooks.com

Printed in U.S.A.
ISBN: 978-1-63727-464-4
Designed by Patricia Frey

All photos courtesy of Iowa State University unless otherwise specified

*To Jack and those who
reach for the baton*

# Contents

## *Part 1: Jack*

## Part 2: The Handoff

# Foreword

JACK TRICE PAVED THE WAY FOR ATHLETES LIKE ME TO REACH THEIR fullest potential. Jack sacrificed so much in order to be a trailblazer for Black college athletes, and his story was a powerful catalyst for change in college athletics. The letter that he wrote the night before his final game in Minnesota displays the immense bravery, humility, and sacrifice that made him the great player and person that he was. College athletics still have a long way to go when it comes to equity, but we have Jack Trice to thank for much of the progress that has been made.

In the letter that he wrote before playing Minnesota, he made it clear that he knew he was going into the lion's den as a Black player who was not welcome on the field. This is a feeling that many Black athletes know all too well. As a Black quarterback, I often felt like my value was questioned in a position usually filled by a White athlete. Although this experience was challenging for me, I know that my experience would have been much more difficult if athletes who came before me, including Jack Trice, had not faced seemingly insurmountable obstacles with extreme courage and strength. This is why it is important for me to pass the torch to younger Black athletes and help them navigate the challenges that they may face and acknowledge the stories and sacrifices that others made before me.

I am thankful for Jack's courage to sacrifice his body, pride, and ultimately his life. His moral strength helped open doors and create opportunities for other college players of color, including me. This college career gave me a chance to compete in the NFL, and I played 10 years as a professional athlete. Jack Trice's career made mine possible. As a football player at Iowa State, I have always felt proud and honored to have played in the only stadium named after a Black man. His story should be known and honored.

—Seneca Wallace, former Iowa State quarterback
and the first African American quarterback to start
a regular-season game for the Green Bay Packers

# Foreword

IT IS SAID THAT 12TH-CENTURY THEOLOGIAN JOHN OF SALISBURY borrowed from Isaac Newton when he wrote: "We are like dwarfs sitting on the shoulders of giants. We see more, and things that are more distant, than they did, not because our sight is superior or because we are taller than they, but because they raise us up, and by their great stature add to ours."

I have no doubt in my mind that Jack Trice fully understood the peril he faced when he represented Iowa State University as the first and only Black member of its football team in 1923.

Denied the opportunity to live on campus with his fellow students, denied the opportunity to room and dine with his teammates on the road, and in some instances his team denied the opportunity to compete against all-White teams that refused to play against a team with a Black player, Jack was undaunted. With tremendous strength of character, grace, and courage, he persevered in circumstances so challenging and even dangerous because he understood that by his great stature, he was adding to all of us who would come after him.

I am indebted to Jack, for he paved the way for me to become the first Black athletic director at Iowa State in 1993. Likewise I am indebted to all the students and faculty members who for more than

20 years lobbied the university's administration to rename Cyclone Stadium in Jack Trice's honor.

In my career as an athletic administrator, which now spans more than 40 years, I count the naming of Jack Trice Stadium at Iowa State University as one of the great privileges in which I have participated.

Jack was a giant of a man. His extraordinary courage raised up so many who came after him. I envision Jack looking down upon his namesake stadium, immensely proud of all the young men whose opportunities to excel are deeply rooted in his courage.

—Eugene Smith, senior vice president and Wolfe Foundation endowed athletic director, The Ohio State University

# Introduction

IN 1923 ANNA TRICE, THE MOTHER OF JOHN "JACK" TRICE, WROTE A LETTER to the president of Iowa State College of Agriculture and Mechanic Arts. In it, she stated: "If there is anything in the life of John Trice and his career that will be an inspiration to the colored students who come to Ames, he has not lived and died in vain. But Mr. President, while I am proud of his honors, he was all I had and I am old and alone. The future is dreary and lonesome."

In such a difficult time, she found solace in a poem, for it must have reminded her of Jack. She enclosed it within the letter:

### THE IDEALIST

He followed his dream and men counted it madness;
He followed his dream up the mountain's steep side;
"See! Here in the valley are music and gladness;
Why then take the highway, the hard way?" they cried.

At length from above them we heard a faint calling;
His scorners turned quickly from feasting and play,
To look toward the mountain height grim and appalling;
"The luck of a fool – he has treasure!" said they.

With ropes and with staves they toiled after, and found him
Midway of the mountain, his treasure outspread;
"Let us share it!" they clamored, pressed rudely around him;
"Take all – it is yours; I go higher," he said.

**—JESSE BROWN POUNDS**

# Part 1

# Jack

*I'm just a Buffalo Soldier*
*In the heart of America*

—BOB MARLEY AND THE WAILERS,
"BUFFALO SOLDIER"

# 1
# A Little Boy with a Big Smile

ON OCTOBER 5, 1923, 21-YEAR-OLD JACK TRICE, ALIVE AND WELL, SAT down to write a letter, its intended recipient unknown. Jack was just a sophomore at Iowa State College, though his pen spoke with a mature wisdom: "My thoughts just before the first real college game of my life. The honor of my race, family and self are at stake. Everyone is expecting me to do big things. I *will*!"

Jack was a star football player, a husband, and a friend. Yet on this night, he found himself alone in a hotel room. As Iowa State's first Black athlete, the color of his skin had separated him from his teammates, as he was forced to eat alone in his room while they dined in the hotel dining room. The quiet around him felt of something greater than himself, and also of something heavy. Jack didn't know it at the time, but in just three short days he would be dead. Although his promising life would be tragically cut short, he would leave a lasting legacy at Iowa State and beyond. The letter he wrote that fateful night would mean different things to different people, but all of them would rally behind it. Never having met Jack, and yet born decades later, they would find his words, and his story, very personal.

With his letter in hand, Jack reached toward a future when athletes and coaches would highlight his sacrificial story "to promote equality in their community." A future when Iowa State would alter its uniform with a patch reminiscent of the stripes on his football jersey. A future when he would inspire a decades-long movement by students to name Iowa State's football stadium after him. It would become college football's first and only major stadium named for an African American. His words would inspire athletes from the walls and echo in the locker room hallway. His name would emblazon the top of the stadium in lights.

Yet his other hand reached backward toward his ancestors, weighed down by centuries of struggle. Those who had come before him had no such honor. Their sacrifice bore no such memorial. As far as the United States was concerned, African Americans had no names.


TO NAME SOMETHING makes it real. It gives it meaning. Before Jack Trice's name was painted on the side of a football stadium, still the only major college football stadium named for an African American, his ancestors were footnotes in a census. The United States of America recorded its census every decade for more than 200 years. But in 1850 and 1860, the names of slaves were not included on the national census of slaves, known as the Slave Schedule. Their names were erased. Instead, census takers simply recorded the name of a slave owner and then the number of slaves he owned and their ages before moving on to the next house.

In 1860 Verban Harrison Trice, a White farmer in west Tennessee, owned 17 slaves, ages 4 to 46. Two of those slaves—Phyllis and Wallace

Trice—were Jack Trice's grandparents. The Trice name was well-known throughout Henderson County. It was a large family that had come from North Carolina around 1822, bringing with them a slave known only as Anaky. Harrison Trice, the patriarch of the Trice family, sired 12 children, many of whom went on to own slaves of their own.

In 1860 the Trice family suffered an unexpected and violent death. Verban's nephew John Harrison Trice was murdered. According to an account recorded at the time by John's brother-in-law and later published in the 1912 *Jackson Sun*, Trice was killed in a struggle with one of his slaves, Jo(e) Harrison. When Jo was arrested, he was asked if he had killed his master. At peace with what he had done, Jo gave one simple reply: "I did."

Following his confession, Jo was convicted of murder and sentenced to hang at the same spot where he and Trice had fought. Before his own life was taken, Jo provided an account of his struggle:

> Me and my master disagreed about the splitting of some rails, and he told me he was going to whip me and tied me with his suspenders.... I walked with him to the head of the hollow, but the suspenders came untied or broke and then we got into a scuffle, during which time I found his knife on the ground, which I took up with my right hand and put my left to his chin and cut his throat from ear to ear at two licks. When he attempted to rise and while on his hands and knees, I thought him not yet dead. I picked up a chunk of wood and struck him on the head, which I concluded would do the work. During the time we scuffled, he told me not to kill him and said if I did, my old master, Trice's father, would hang me. He begged me twice to quit and called a little boy, Frank, to come there.

I waited some three or four minutes, and before he was quite dead, I took him upon my shoulder with his head to my back, walked down the hollow, through a skirt of woods in the farm, to the opposite side, crossing five fences, during which I did not stop nor rest, except at one lone fence I let him fall. When outside I walked straight to the road leading from his house to Esq. Fry's, laid him down by the side of it, and then took him by the feet and dragged him about ten steps upon his face. I then laid his hat and some corn by the road in order that when he was found no one would think the deed was done on the side of the farm upon which I worked.

It was in the crucible between Jo Harrison's death and the dawn of emancipation that Jack's father, Green, was born to Phyllis and Wallace. It was 1864, and the Civil War had raged for three years. Abraham Lincoln had already signed the Emancipation Proclamation and the Union Army was occupying Tennessee. Andrew Johnson, the acting governor of Tennessee, had proclaimed that the Black men and women of his state were no longer bound by slavery. And yet Green and his parents were not free.

Freedom did not officially come to Phyllis Trice and her infant son until the following year, when Johnson became Lincoln's vice president and Tennessee became the first Confederate state to formally abolish slavery. Wallace was no longer with them. He may have been sold off or died. His name no longer appeared in any records. Phyllis no longer had a husband.

Despite their newfound freedom, Phyllis—who was penniless and unable to read or write—and Green continued living on Verban's farm. For the next few years, Phyllis worked in his house, and she and Green lived in their old slave quarters. Legal slavery had ended, but many still struggled with economic uncertainty.

Verban died in 1873, and without a will, his trust and farm passed to his son James. With nothing left but a forced family name, Phyllis and Green—who was nine years old—left the Trice farm. Many emancipated slaves in the area had turned to sharecropping as a means of financial support. In exchange for renting a small portion of land, they gave up a percentage of their crop to the local landowner, who was usually a White former slave owner.

By 1880 Green had reached his teenage years and was living with and working for a young Black farmer named G. Cogdell. Phyllis was living nearby in another house with Green's brother and helping in the fields. Two years later, on the morning of April 6, 1882, the *Public Ledger* posted the headline BAD DARKY. In the brief article, the paper reported that a drunken stonecutter had been lured into a riverfront den and robbed by several people. After taking his money, the assailants had forced the victim out onto the road and ordered him to leave. The local police got word of the matter, and upon visiting the area, they found one Green Trice, a "darky with a lantern in his hand."

Green was taken to the station and searched. No money was found, but nevertheless, he was sentenced to 40 days in prison on "general principles." A pistol had been found in the young Black man's pocket by the arresting officer. The same paper reported on the conditions of another dark-skinned man who suffered a similar fate that very night. The unnamed Black man was found "prowling about after midnight," apparently a common occurrence because a recent flood had dispersed many Black families from their homes. In court, the judge—looking down over the rim of his glasses—inquired to the defendant, "Don't you know we close this town up at 12:00?" And per his usual routine on these matters, he ended the encounter by imploring the Black defendant to ensure that others heeded his message.

By the fall of that year, 18-year-old Green had decided he could no longer stay in Tennessee. He needed to leave the South. He wanted to travel west to join the U.S. military. There, his only master would be the U.S. government. In doing so, he ended up fighting for the same country that had both enslaved and later freed his parents. His journey across the country took him to Fort Davis, Texas. There, on November 21, 1882, he enlisted in the 10th US Cavalry, L Company. Even at that time, the 10th unit was better known by its more common name, the Buffalo Soldiers.

The Buffalo Soldiers had earned their name from the local Native Americans who saw the Black men on the field of battle. At first, the Native Americans were drawn to the superficial features of the Black soldiers—curly black hair that reminded them of the buffalo. But over time, the strength of the fight in the men, like that of the sacred creature, imbued the moniker with greater meaning.

L Company did not see much direct action, but they were entrusted with guarding stagecoaches filled with mail and other cargo traveling on the western roads of Texas and Arizona. Their job was to keep hostile tribes and robbers at bay. Later, as a football player, Jack would do the same. He would block the enemy's advance so his football team could take territory from them across the gridiron. He readily put his body on the line for the benefit of those around him.

One chance encounter in the military left Green with a scar on his hand and a story to tell. It became one of Jack's favorites. Green's unit was surrounded by Native Americans hostile to its mission. The wagons encircling their camp had been set on fire. The soldiers could see no way out. Flames and thick smoke blocked their escape. As the wall of fire grew, Private Green thought to himself that his "time was up." Fortunately, the captain did some quick thinking. He ordered a backfire be built from the center to alter the course of the advancing flames. The men snapped into action, piling up what wood and other flammable materials they could muster. The plan worked. The circle of flames grew in front of them, but behind them it began to break. It gave them just enough time and space to block the enemy. They jumped over the opening in the flames, escaping with what little they could grab, and their lives.

Five years passed, and Green's service contract was complete. He applied for a formal discharge and pension on December 5, 1887. He came into contact with Wallace J. Ford, who offered work on a farm he had just purchased along the northern border of Ohio in a small town called Hiram. There weren't many people there, and practically no Black folks, but it was good money and provided a roof over his head. Green accepted the offer and traveled with Wallace and his wife, Mary, to Hiram, ready to start a new life on the Ford farm.

By the time Green began working for Wallace, the older White man was nearing his 70s. Wallace carried his head with a distinctive tilt, thought to be a consequence of an accident when he was 21 years old. Early one morning, while traveling with a doctor on a westward quest to explore California and the Pacific coast, Wallace had left their camp in the early hours of the morning to walk along the water. The rest of his party was still fast asleep. Upon returning to camp, the doctor mistook Wallace for an intruder and shot him in the face with the Colt revolver that was laying by his side. The bullet took Wallace's eye and part of his left ear, although according to the doctor's account, the young Ohioan's reaction was "no more than stunned."

Wallace carried significant weight in the small town of Hiram. He was a local politician who had been personal secretary to his close friend and future U.S. president James Garfield. The Ford family was well-known across the Western Reserve. They had built their name through farming, banking, and politics. Still, despite the growth of the family's coffers, Wallace and the other boys in the Ford family were raised under the auspices of "rigid discipline" and the "tuition of constant labor," They were taught at a young age to measure their accomplishments only by "such as were made for themselves by personal endeavor."

Religion was an important cornerstone of life on the Ford farm. Wallace's parents were among the early Disciples of Christ—the Protestant group that had founded Hiram. The Disciples later established Hiram College in 1850, which became the de facto geographical and economic center of the town. Green, and soon Jack, would walk in the shadow of the campus bell tower. Its spire could be easily spotted above the surrounding athletic fields, YMCA, hardware stores, and town hotel. With the college at its nexus, a square mile extended outward in all directions, defining Hiram Village proper.

Green and Wallace attended services inside of the church, surrounded by 18 individual stained-glass windows depicting the men and women who had played important roles in the town's history, including James Garfield. The young township where Jack would be born was becoming known as much for its many cattle farms as it was its cheese factories. Mills and other industrial factories popped up along its rivers.

Settling in Hiram, Green found himself caught between both geographical and cultural crosscurrents. While Ohio's northern border is defined by the Lake Erie coastline across from Canada, the state's southern border runs along 436 miles of former slave states. As a result, strong color lines still existed in the state even decades after the Civil War. They "lessened" slightly as one moved northward, but they in no way disappeared.

At the time, progressive economies were pulling people of color north toward Cleveland, while the cultural reconstruction of the South sought to weigh them down. Hiram's own meandering water supply was itself a reflection of the crosscurrents flowing through Ohio. The western rivers of the township coursed northward along the Cuyahoga River into Lake Erie, while the waters of the Mahoning River along the eastern part permeated south toward the Gulf of Mexico. As a rising Black football star from a small White town, Jack would also find himself caught between two crosscurrents.

Hiram joined the electrical grid in 1894. Meanwhile, the rest of Ohio in the 1890s was struggling with a wave of lynchings. It rose to such a level that embarrassing comparisons to the South had begun. In an attempt to stave off a similar spiral, a bill was introduced in the Ohio state assembly to allow families of lynching victims to sue for monetary damages. Financial consequences, it seemed, were one of the best available defenses against the killing of unarmed Black men. The bill was named the Smith Act, after Harry Smith, the African American state representative who had championed it.

Hiram's everyday life reinforced its identity as a small town of shared values where, come Sunday morning, everyone would be headed in the same direction. Like a black hole or the sun, the church at the center of town bent everyone's orbits. Being that fellow townsperson were headed the same way, they might even take the stroll together. It didn't matter whether you were a farmer or a student of the ministry, your paths would merge.

Green quickly became an active member of the Hiram community. Often on his way to church, he came across two young White boys he knew. Without hesitation, he would take one under each arm and usher them to Sunday school. In fact, Green was well-known to all the families with young children in Hiram.

Since he was in his early 20s and had no formal education outside of that needed for various job responsibilities, Green decided to enter the first grade. Like the kids in his class, Green played outside during recess. The children used his arms as swings. Next to the schoolhouse, he became a giant black silhouette, arms extended outward like a cross, with little White children playing under them.

By 1900, when he was 36, Green began renting his own land to farm. As his own roots were growing deeper into Hiram, he brought his younger brother, Lee, from Tennessee and found him work as a hired hand for Ford. In April of that year Green married Anna Wilcoxson.

Anna had been born in Virginia but by age 11 was already living in Hiram with her parents, siblings, niece, and two nephews. Her father was a local laborer and her mother attended to the needs of the household—"keeping house" as they referred to it. When the Wilcoxson family had moved to Hiram, the only other Black people in town were Lucy Richards, a light-skinned 50-year-old woman with French heritage who was married to a 76-year-old White clockmaker, and John McLard, a 36-year-old laborer from Tennessee.

Two years after Green and Anna were married, on May 12, 1902, John "Jack" Trice was born. With the addition of Jack, the Trice family members made up more than half of the Black population of Hiram. In a town of more than 650 people, there were still only seven Black people in town, and four of them, including Lee, were Trices.

In 1907, when Jack was five years old, telephone lines were erected in Hiram for the first time, connecting it with nearby cities. That same year, Jack met his childhood friend Gaylord Bates. Gaylord moved to Hiram with his family from New York City. His father, Miner Lee Bates, had been the pastor of the First Church of the Disciples. Miner was a "forceful, convincing, and eloquent" clergyman and was tapped as the next president of Hiram College.

Jack was a little boy with a big smile. Although he was the only Black kid in Hiram, his parents made sure he attended classes at one of the local schools. Since the rooms at the school were often used to house two grades at a time, Jack shared the classroom with Gaylord, who was one year ahead of him. Despite their differences in circumstances, Gaylord later recalled in 1956 to the Hiram County Historical Society that Jack led his young life with "a hearty good humor that made him indistinguishable from his schoolmates." Jack attended school parties at the local White people's homes where, as children, Gaylord and his friends never had "a thought of any difference of color of skin." It was with them that Jack played sports, attended Boy Scouts meetings, and went to Sunday school. Jack did his best to fit in and was "as full of fun and practical jokes as anyone else."

Yet Jack's childhood in the small town was marked by an unforeseen and lasting tragedy. Three months before Jack's seventh birthday, his father died. Like Green before him, Jack found himself without a father—and Anna was without a husband. Green's sudden death at only 45 years old was a shock to the community. Lee was called back from a trip to Tennessee. Wallace and Mary Ford traveled down to Hiram from Trumbull, which lay north along Lake Erie, to honor their former farmhand. They joined Jack and Anna in mourning Greene's passing.

An obituary ran in the local paper asserting to all who read it that Green's life was "worthy of more than a passing notice." It noted that Green, born of Black parents, had known "every form of poverty— hunger, rags, cold, often without home, friend, or shelter." And yet, it said, he scarcely alluded to his days of hardship, focusing instead on bettering himself and those around him.

Because he had been "one of [Hiram's] most dependable citizens" for 20 years, the predominantly White town honored Green, the son of freed slaves who had fought with the Buffalo Soldiers and found solid work as a farmer. The tight-knit community came together for a large public funeral. Green was remembered as honest, industrial, capable, and frugal. As President Bates was out of town preaching, the service was overseen by Rev. Edmund Wakefield, the former president of Hiram College. That day Green Trice was declared "an honor to his race."

Most people attributed the death of Green Trice to a heart attack. His death certificate, however, stated the cause of death was uremia. In other words, he suffered from a deadly buildup of poisonous toxins in the body. The usual source of this condition is kidney failure—a disease that still today has a predilection for Black bodies.

Unyielding to tragedy, Anna chose to raise Jack by herself, instilling in him the importance of education and hard work. She filed for a widow's army pension and purchased a home in Hiram Village, closer to the center of town. To help make ends meet, she rented a room to a lodger, Lovel Willson, a widowered 87-year-old traveling salesman from Massachusetts. Anna worked as a dressmaker and also as a cook with her sister at the Commons, where the male college students ate their meals.

According to Gaylord, Anna had a "wisdom and dignity about her" that was respected by the women of Hiram. She was known as a strong and determined woman, and therefore, when it came to Jack, she "had little time to cater to his whims." Discipline was important, and while she gave Jack plenty of time to play with his friends, she "insisted that certain chores be done at her convenience and not his." Like any other boy in the town when he had chores to do, Jack would try to escape outside the house to play ball with the rest of the kids. Once his absence was discovered, a wave of dejection would come across his face—and sadistic pleasure would appear on his friends' faces—when in a scene familiar in small towns everywhere, "his mother's voice would boom out to call him back to work and break up a ball game." Jack's childish devilry did not go unpunished. As was the custom of the time, if he failed to heed his mother's instruction, he would be "occasionally spanked or whipped." His fellow children judged the ensuing "crocodile tears and cries of pain were as spirited as any," according to a later account from Gaylord.

As Jack grew older, the stark reality of being the only Black boy in a predominantly White town made itself known. Although still younger than them, he was not immune to the jokes and "pointed remarks of college students with respect to his race." Jack learned to find strength deep inside himself—an armor against the sharp barbs about his race. As the son of the college president and Jack's childhood friend, Gaylord recalled seeing these interactions play out. Studying him for a response, he would only see Jack maintain his "good grace and if he became angry maintained perfect self-control."

By the time Jack had finished eighth grade and was ready for high school, Anna had concluded that her son was living too sheltered a life in Hiram. At 60 years old, Hiram College had been attracting those from as far as Japan interested in higher education and quiet repose. Nestled in the bucolic Western Reserve, it was advertised as both "healthful and free of distractions." As such, the distraction-free town was socially and culturally isolated compared to its much larger neighbor, Cleveland. The relative Midwest metropolis was just a few years away from becoming the fifth-largest city in the U.S. and loomed only 30 miles away, reachable in 10 stops by streetcar.

Anna knew what it was like to grow up in Hiram, for she herself had done so. She wanted Jack to "be better prepared for maturity" and felt their small town could not provide that for him. The spring after Green's death, his brother, Lee, had married Pearl Reno, an eighteen-year-old musician from Mississippi. The two moved in with her family in suburban Solon, just outside Cleveland. A few years later, the young couple moved into the bustling city, where Lee found work as a garbage collector. Their home was filled with two sons of their own (and another would soon be on the way), but Anna knew they would make room for their nephew Jack.

Anna thought living with Lee and Pearl in the bigger city might present Jack with the opportunity "to make social contacts with people of his own race." In fact, the Black population of Cleveland had begun to grow significantly during the early stages of the Great Migration, which would see nearly six million African Americans move northward from the South to places such as Chicago, Detroit, and Cleveland.

The move to Cleveland would provide Jack a life among more people of color than he could experience back in Hiram. However, as Jack would soon learn, even in Cleveland his presence could still be something of an oddity. Green had left his mother as a teenager and found a home with the Buffalo Soldiers standing shoulder to shoulder with other proud African American men. Jack too would leave his hometown as a teenager and find himself standing proudly shoulder to shoulder among his own little army. But in Jack's case, his was a lone Black face.

# 2
# Sad Sam and East Tech Football

JACK'S ADOLESCENCE MIRRORED THE ADOLESCENCE OF FOOTBALL itself. As Jack matured, so did the sport of football in America. It had not yet reached professional adulthood, but it had entered its rebellious teenage years in Ohio.

As Jack was getting ready to leave Hiram for Cleveland, in Canton—about 50 miles south of Hiram—Sam Williams was lining up along the left end of the offensive line. The muscles of his face formed the ever-present frown that had earned him his nickname, "Sad" Sam. It was four minutes into the 1917 Ohio League professional championship game, and Sam's team was on the 1-yard line of their archrival, the Massillon Tigers. The snowfall was beginning to quicken. Williams tensed up right before the ball was snapped. Quickly he surged forward, blocking the oncoming defender. Off to his right, he could see the team's star halfback, Jim Thorpe, punch through the hole in the middle of the defense for the game's first touchdown. The Ohio crowd cheered its approval, unaware of the secret before them.

What the fans didn't know was that there was an impostor on the field. One of the men they cheered for wasn't who he said he was. Sam Williams didn't exist. In reality, Williams was Sam Willaman, the lauded former All–Ohio State halfback. During the week Willaman was the head football coach at the school Jack was about to attend, East Technical High School in Cleveland, whose team was the Carpenters. But on Sunday afternoons, he was Sam Williams, the starting end for the 1916 defending champion Canton Bulldogs.

The Bulldogs were part of the professional football Ohio League. Football at the time was undergoing a metamorphosis. Up until 1905, football was primarily played between Ivy League universities. Professional football existed only in small, regional organizations. Further, the game's lack of coherent rules had set it on a path toward abolishment, even among universities.

In 1905, 18 players died and many others suffered significant injuries. Charles Eliot, the president of Harvard University had led the charge to outlaw football. Eliot, himself a boxer, was an advocate of personal fitness. One of his early goals as university president was to improve the general well-being and physique of the young Harvard men on campus. Team sports, however, represented somewhat of a conundrum to the influential academic. He saw them as creating an unnecessary distraction on campus. In addition, they provided young men with an opportunity to cheat or exploit weaknesses. A curveball in baseball, for example, was an act of deceit. Finding a hole in the other team's football line would be less honorable than attacking their strongest fortification.

A turning point in football's history occurred in 1905 when a 46-year-old Harvard graduate invited the coaches of Harvard, Yale, and Princeton to the White House for a meeting on the state of the game. President Teddy Roosevelt had been a fan of football ever since, as an 18-year-old freshman, he had attended the second-ever Harvard-Yale football game. At the lunchtime meeting that fall day, the president of the United States challenged the men to transform the sport for the better. In response, they listened and acted. That meeting prompted several rule changes, including allowing the forward pass, which opened up and spread out the field of play. First downs were increased from five to ten yards. And a line of scrimmage was laid down to separate the offensive and defensive lines before the play began.

In 1917, in his third year in the league, Sam Willaman found himself on the defending champion Canton Bulldogs alongside a true multisport star, Jim Thorpe. Jim had won Olympic gold in both the pentathlon and decathlon and played in the World Series for the New York Giants. The Massillon Tigers had won the 1915 championship, but bolstered by Thorpe, the Bulldogs had won the 1916 championship resoundingly. That meant 1917 would be the rubber match for the two teams. The Tigers were led by Charles Brickley, a Harvard graduate who had a strong kicking leg. Prior to the Canton matchup, he had booted several goals from farther than 55 yards. This led to the Tigers-Bulldogs game being touted as Brickley vs. Thorpe. Thorpe may have had pure athleticism on his side, but Brickley had Harvard-educated cunning. He also had Knute Rockne.

Rockne was a shrewd strategist and brought with him the Notre Dame Shift and several trick plays. Norway-born Rockne had emigrated to the United States with his parents when he was five years old. He learned to play football in the Logan Square neighborhood of northwest Chicago. At the age of 22, Rockne had saved enough money for college and enrolled at Notre Dame.

It was there, as running back, offensive end, and the team captain that the young Norwegian had a key hand in transforming the game of football. Prior to Rockne's involvement, the forward pass was illegal but had been underutilized. In 1913 against West Point, the Fighting Irish launched an aerial assault on the Cadets the likes of which had never been seen. The quarterback was still a relatively new position in football, but that didn't stop the Irish's Charles Dorais from connecting with Rockne for two 50-yard bombs, leading their team downfield to take the lead. Dorais finished the game with seemingly modern statistics: 14-for-17 passing attempts, 243 yards throwing, and three touchdowns. Both Dorais and Rockne continued to highlight the passing game and finished their collegiate careers as All-Americans. Upon graduating, they took their aerial act to the next level in the Ohio League.

Rockne's tactics and on-field running maneuvers helped power the Tigers to the 1915 Ohio League championship. And the next year, the Bulldogs won, setting up the aforementioned 1917 rubber match between Rockne's team and Willaman's. In a game filled with snow and shenanigans—including a fistfight and an entire second platoon composed of a local Ambulance Corps—Thorpe, Willaman, and the Bulldogs won the game 14–0. Following the 1917 season, the realities of America and the world beyond football prevented the 1918 season from reaching its full potential. Resources and men were directed toward World War I. That fall also saw the deadliest second wave of the 1918 Spanish Flu, leaving 200,000 dead in October alone and severely limiting travel within the country.

Thorpe returned the next year, in 1919, to lead the Bulldogs to a third consecutive championship. He also helped lead the charge through the dawn of the nationally organized American Professional Football Association. It was the seedling of today's National Football League. Knute Rockne left professional football to take over the head football coaching position at his alma mater, Notre Dame. There he began one of the greatest coaching careers in the history of college football. It would not be the last time he and Sam Willaman would have competing interests when it came to football. And it would not be the last time Rockne's name would be brought up in the story of Jack Trice. Willaman also left professional football to focus on coaching full-time at East Tech. There, two new students and best friends would lash their young destinies to his.

ACCORDING TO THE 1940 "Study of Cleveland's Negro Areas," the Colored Belt of Cleveland ran between Cedar Avenue on the north, the Nickel Plate Road on the east and the south, and Central Avenue and East 9th Street on its west. The lower part of this section was already notably congested even before it saw an influx of Black families. Within the Colored Belt, there were 10 social centers, 15 playgrounds, and 2 bathhouses. There were 75 poolrooms, with the establishments in the lower section predominantly owned by people of color. By the mid-to-late 1920s, there were 15 movie theaters showing moving pictures. Several of these theaters outlawed popcorn and Black patrons. Popcorn was frowned upon in movie theaters because it was considered too noisy and disruptive. No reason was given for the other rule.

A handful of dance halls were scattered across the Colored Belt, a remnant of the area's former German population. Education was a growing pillar of the community. According to "Facts About the Colored Population of Cleveland" which summarized a 1924 survey by Rev. John Prucha, of the 30,000 people of color aged 10 years or older, 94.2 percent were literate. This was in contrast to only 87 percent of foreign-born residents, comprising mainly Italians, Russians, Poles, and Czecho-Slovaks. Like many other growing metropolitan American cities, many of the Eastern European immigrants were Jewish and, along with the Italians, interacted with and lived in close proximity to the Black community. It was reported that despite the barriers of the 1920s, within the Colored Belt alone there were 32 doctors, 23 attorneys, 17 dentists, 10 pharmacists, 5 graduate nurses, and more than 236 college graduates of color.

A few middle-class Black families sought refuge outside the density of the Colored Belt in outlying Cleveland neighborhoods such as Mount Pleasant and Glenville. These early integrated enclaves provided more space and freestanding houses that better resembled the upwardly mobile neighborhoods found outside the Colored Belt. The trade-off, however, was that Black families were significantly outnumbered and therefore had less political sway in their neighborhoods to gain access to places such as swimming pools, something they could have obtained in the more densely stacked Colored Belt.

Prior to Jack's arrival, his Uncle Lee and Aunt Pearl had found a house in Mount Pleasant. It was the fastest-growing cluster of Black-owned homes outside of the Colored Belt but still only represented 5 percent of the African American population in Cleveland. Railroad workers were the area's first Black residents, in the early 1900s. When their employer went bankrupt, they were paid in land rather than missed wages. Growth in the area was slow initially, but by 1907, a Black real estate agent with the auspicious name of Welcome T. Blue was advertising lots for as low as $200. Many of his advertisements included phrases such as, "Get Away From the Crowded Smoky City. Own Your Own Home. Raise Garden Fruit. Chickens, Hogs, Cows" and "100 Afro-American Families Live There Today."

Cleveland suburbs historian Todd Michney noted this was likely a sales-pitch exaggeration and the real number of Black families living in Mount Pleasant at the time was likely closer to 25. The chicken and hogs, however, were not a marketing ploy. Several of the homes in the area did have hog pens and chicken coops. Being able to produce their own food was important to newly settled Black families who had not owned a home before. Cows too could be found grazing on the large empty lots between houses. An occasional pony provided rides for the neighborhood children. The houses themselves were often haphazardly designed. Many provided a roof for two families and included a workshop or even a second house on the back lot. The scene looked very rural. Only the main Kinsman Road was paved, while the remaining streets were made of "country blacktop."

The area north of Kinsman between East 126th and 130th became the landing ground for middle-class Black families in Mount Pleasant. Many had migrated from the South in search of economic stability and found its promise in middle and upper working-class positions. Several of them lived in two-story homes on Lee and Pearl's street, East 128th St. They found work as carpenters, drivers, and chefs, among other things. Mount Pleasant was in the midst of undergoing a metamorphosis from farmland and orchards into dirt plots for building upon.

The area was also home to a large Jewish population, followed by Italians and Hungarians, who were moving out of the crowded urban downtown area in search of more suburban middle-class neighborhoods. They sought refuge from the crushing crowds and rising downtown rents.

Jack arrived in February 1917 and enrolled at East Technical High School (at that time, students could start in the fall or winter). It was the first public trade school located in Cleveland and had first opened its doors at 7:30 AM on the crisp autumn morning of October 12, 1908, the year after Jack lost his father. The school building was a four-story Gothic-inspired edifice that rose to a dramatic peak at its center. The brick and terra-cotta facade featured rows of partly translucent windows. Inside, its walls were coated with a plaster that peeled slightly more with each year.

The school—which housed a massive 25 percent of Cleveland's high school students—was located on the corner of East 55th and Scoville Ave. Its location was purposefully chosen to allow easy access from all parts of the city. It had the additional benefit of abutting the manufacturing district but still stood far enough away that faculty and students could breathe free from the "smoke and grime" of the industry. The school represented the "inauguration" of a new idea to Cleveland, one whose purpose was to provide instruction to large numbers of boys and girls who were otherwise "hitherto doomed by social and economic conditions to the slavery that is the inevitable, and apparently, unavoidable lot of the unskilled worker." By training these young men and women, they could fulfill important, and therefore well-paid, roles within the industrial complex of the city.

Besides the usual academic requirements, boys were offered classes in agriculture, machine shop, mechanical drawing, and metalworking. Girls were offered stenography, trade sewing, and domestic science. The school was quick to adopt the burgeoning fields of automobile work and theatrical crafts with an eye toward adding aeronautics. For those students with their lofty sights set on college, classes were offered in German, the language of mechanics at the time, and upper-level mathematics. Monday through Friday, the hum of chatter within the student-filled hallways would be overpowered by the sounds of band saws whirring and printing presses clanking. The smells of scorched wood and hot metal wafted up the stairs, taking their four-year lease within young nostrils.

By the time Jack first walked up the front steps of East Technical High School in 1917, many of its new grads had already left Cleveland and flown across the ocean with the intention of using their newly acquired engineering skills fighting in World War I. Recent East Tech grads eagerly wrote back home, where their tales of training were published in the pages of the *June Bug* yearbook for underclassmen to read. They pointed out that in the military, trigonometry and French were replaced by classes on grenade throwing and trench warfare. Nevertheless, East Tech, they declared, had prepared them admirably for the Great War.

Back home the war effort pervaded all aspects of life, and students did what they could to help. Jack's first month at school was marked by fundraising efforts, including Thrift Stamp drives and Liberty Bond purchases. With the fight in Europe garnering everyone's attention, the freshman class entered largely unnoticed. The "flats," as underclassmen were called, spent most of their time trying to figure out which set of stairs to take to class, and often found the teachers were not the ones to ask. A running hallway joke was that freshmen would believe any directions you told them, even if you told them their basement classes were on the fourth floor.

By the fall of 1918, the Spanish Flu had found its way to Cleveland. Although on October 7 the mayor reassured everyone the situation was under control, by October 9 more than 500 new cases had emerged in the city. On October 10, based on new reports, more radical mitigation steps were deemed necessary. The mayor declared that all social and religious gatherings would need to be limited. The first wave of closings began on October 14, including theaters, movie houses, dance halls, and churches. Saloons, poolrooms, and cabarets were not included in the first wave of orders because officials at the time believed the crowds there were not large enough to be a significant risk of transmission.

Schools were initially kept open because it was felt that students could be better monitored in the classroom than at home. As long as student absentee rates did not climb up to 20 percent of enrollment, each school could remain open. Beyond that, a school would have to close. If the overall absentee rate for all schools combined reached 10 percent of total enrollment, then the entire Cleveland school system would have to shut its doors and all students would have to stay home.

Eventually, as the flu continued its spread, business hours downtown were reduced and only essential services, such as telegraph offices and drugstores, remained fully open. Business owners protested but ultimately complied. All open-air gatherings were prohibited after sundown, and any gatherings during the day required preapproval. It was feared that Cleveland hospitals would soon run out of beds.

According to the Influenza Archive, by October 15 schools were closed and teachers were being used as nurses and contact tracers. Schools were canceled for a six-week "influenza vacation." The powers that be combated initial reluctance with the idea that if too many young men fell ill, they wouldn't be around to fight the war overseas. It became a patriotic duty to stay home if you had symptoms, though not all citizens complied. Several arrests of people flouting the rules were made at religious gatherings, card games, cigar stores, and candy shops.

By the middle of November, the pandemic was beginning to wane. Businesses began reopening and schools started back up again. In just five months, 3.5 percent of the city's population had come down with influenza or pneumonia, and of those who became symptomatic, 16 percent had died.

As school resumed, so did extracurricular activities. Students attended classes during the day and joined junior and senior clubs after school. Among the many clubs at East Tech, including debate and drama, 1918 saw the establishment of the S.O.S. club, a group of twenty girls whose job it was to attend sports games, sell tickets, and organize rallies. To be admitted, a female student had to be a junior or senior and receive a two-thirds approval vote by her peers. Initiation rituals also found their way into student clubs, where unsuspecting sophomores would turn the corner of a hallway to find their junior counterparts dressed as pirates in bright bandannas dragging red doll-filled wagons behind them, waiting to ceremoniously welcome the newcomers into the organization. Jack hadn't yet made it to the level of the varsity team and S.O.S. cheers, which were reserved for upperclassmen, but it was on the freshman football team that he first met one of his greatest supporters, Johnny Behm.

Johnny was a red-haired boy with a mischievous streak, and everyone called him Red. Standing next to Jack offered a distinct visual contrast, as Johnny was only 5'7", clearly smaller than Jack, who stood over six feet tall. As incoming members of the freshman football club, Jack weighed more than 170 pounds (and would quickly grow to nearly 200). Johnny, on the other hand, weighed in at only 130 pounds. What Johnny lacked in size on the field, however, he more than made up for with agility. It was a trait surpassed only by his confidence (one example: he claimed to have lost at checkers only once in his life).

Even then football was a major draw in Ohio, and high school football was no different. East Tech was surrounded by several local rivals in what was—and still is—known as the Senate Athletic League. As the East Tech football coach, Sam Willaman had already begun to build the school's reputation for a high-level football program. He would run college-level plays with the high schoolers, focusing on a system that centered on "every man getting his man" during the game. In all but one year from 1915 to 1919, East Tech stood atop or was tied for the pinnacle of the Senate League, but the borders of its reign always stopped outside the Cleveland Metropolitan School District.

Running interference to allow open passes was a cornerstone of their offense, and it required someone with size and speed to lead the charge—someone such as Jack Trice. By the time Jack and Johnny Behm were juniors at East Tech, they had become best friends and were beginning the football season that would help define their futures. As a junior Jack was considered by many to be "undoubtedly the best tackle that ever played" for East Tech. He had speed, strength, and smarts. Johnny, meanwhile, was already on his way to becoming a rare four-sport high school star. He was one of the three legendary Behm brothers, who garnered weekly headlines in the local *Cleveland Plain Dealer*. There was also Norton Behm—known as Norty or Mope—who was a year older than Johnny but was in the same grade. He was the team's halfback, and their brother, Art, laid claim to the local golf links.

Jack's star began to rise in his junior year, and the rest of the class of 1922 "discovered" East Tech not only had a football team but a team that carried with it some importance. To the students, the football games became a welcome respite following turbulent war years that included both military drills and infection-control training. According to Jack's senior yearbook, it became both his "smile and his tackle" that lent the students weekly comfort. Suddenly football at East Tech held a teenager's interest just as much as mixers filled with popcorn balls and doughnuts. The games were more boisterous than pretending to get "touched" on apple cider. And no matter the social construct of the day, even Jack—irrespective of the color of his skin—could take part in these festivities. He could even play a starring role.

Besides Jack and the Behm brothers, the team featured senior-year quarterback Bert Berkowitz, known in the yearbook for his "good nature" as much as for his passing arm. He was from a Jewish family, and his father had emigrated from Hungary. Joining them was the aptly named Champ Hardy, the future senior class and homeroom president, who was just as comfortable on the field as he was in Electrical Club or in his role as vice president of the Hi-Y club. (On paper, Hi-Y was meant to bring together local high school boys of the

Young Men's Christian Association, its "specific purpose to establish high standards of Christian character among the boys.")

According to the East Tech Yearbook, each week, the local girls would cook dinner for the boys and then would provide the evening's wholesome entertainment, such as a lecture on what their "ideal boy" would be. Afterward, their male counterparts would retire to a classroom with the instructions to discuss the multifaceted problems of school and society, with the Bible as the background. One such evening was described in the 1922 *June Bug* yearbook. There you might find Johnny Behm and Champ Hardy, whose senior yearbook marked him as "sure to succeed," sauntering into the local YMCA classroom and pulling themselves up to the meeting table. Johnny would be swiftly rebuked for propping his "number 11s" onto the table. The worn shoes would momentarily disappear from view before returning to the surface of the table. The club president would then follow with his weekly request for dues that were outstanding. The usual groans would be capitalized by the clinking of a so-called "Chinese nickel" being slid across the table. The coin with the hole in the middle would be promptly returned to its known owner, Champ Hardy.

With the opening formalities dispensed, the topic of discussion would move toward the debate of the evening, such as whether or not girls should smoke. After a vigorous hour of back-and-forth, Champ would rise up and walk toward the door, offering to the floor a "move we make a motion." All other voices would chorus agreement, marking the end of the meeting.

Rounding out Jack's football circle was Herbert Carlson, nicknamed "Swede" for his family heritage. His Viking genetics were well advertised in his size and strength. Jack held the school record for heaving the iron ball of the shot put, but the light-haired Swede preferred setting his own school record with a spear-tipped javelin.

EACH WEEKEND OF that 1920 East Tech football season provided a new wave of opportunity for Jack and his teammates. Together, under the guidance of Sam Willaman, they had their sights set on winning the Senate League. The outcome of each box score would either breathe more wind into their sails or leave them dead in the water. What follows is a week-by-week rundown of the season. It was a journey made not only by Jack, but his teammates ands friends, too.

## September 25 vs. Lakewood

The football season kicked off on September 25. East Tech's first opponent was Lakewood High School, hailing from the fast-growing Lakewood suburb just west of Cleveland. Despite being one of the smaller teams of the league, the brown-and-gold East Tech came out looking larger than their suburban opponents. The team played on neutral ground at their rival West Tech's field. Champ Hardy crouched at center. Bert Berkowitz lined up behind him in the quarterback spot. Swede Carlson filled up the space of the forward slot. The right side was composed of Johnny, Norty, and Jack. The referee blew his whistle, and East Tech's season was officially under way.

The first scoring play began with Berkowitz running for 20 yards following a handoff. Then Carlson (in those days anybody could throw the ball) threw a pass to Norty Behm, who carried the ball over the goal line. East Tech's second touchdown came after a long bomb that put the ball on the Lakewood 2-yard line. Carlson used his size to push the ball forward on the play for the score.

In the third quarter, Berkowitz broke free for a 30-yard run to the end zone, but it was called back because East Tech had a player offside. East Tech was unable to score any more touchdowns but easily defeated Lakewood 12–0.

## October 2 vs. Lincoln

East Tech's second game, against small-town Lincoln High School, proved even easier. As the calendar page turned to October, Johnny Behm, Berkowitz, Carlson, and McFarland, the halfback on the left side, combined for 12 touchdowns in an 84–0 blowout.

## October 9 vs. Glenville

The following week, most of the city's attention was focused on the Cleveland Indians. Over the course of seven games, the Indians snatched the 1920 World Series from the Brooklyn Dodgers (aka the Robins). East Tech quietly won this game against Glenville 28–0.

## October 16 vs. Shaw

With three games under their belt, the East Tech team squared off against Shaw from East Cleveland. This time Willaman's team showed off a big passing game, still something relatively new to the game of football. Jack and the other blockers kept the pressure on with a rapidly moving forward offense. Berkowitz scored two, and Carlson, Johnny, Norty, and McFarland had one TD each. Berkowitz and Johnny were called the stars of the game by the local press. The team blanked Shaw 42–0.

## October 23 vs. East High

Two days after their victory over Shaw, the local paper considered East Tech the likely Senate League best but suggested their game against East High would be their first true litmus test, as East High was also considered a top contender. The top three undefeated leaders of the league were West Tech, East Tech, and East High. By the time the East High game came to a close, the Carpenters of East Tech made a resounding statement, soundly defeating their previously undefeated opponent 49–0.

## October 29 vs. Longwood

After victories in Week 5, East Tech and West Tech found themselves perched atop the Senate League with a perfect record of 4–0. (East Tech had won five games, but since Shaw was not part of the Senate League, its Senate League record was exactly the same as West Tech's.) The *Cleveland Plain dealer* considered the rest of teams in the league "merely props in the cast" on the way to the inevitable showdown between the league rivals. East Tech continued flying high against Longwood, beating them 102–0 despite the game being shortened to seven-minute quarters. West Tech also won their game of the week 47–7, which was notable considering the second string and scrubs played half the game.

## November 5 vs. Saint Ignatius

As November began, East Tech boasted a record 275 points in five Senate League games, and not a single opponent had reached their end zone. East Tech wasn't expecting much of a fight from their next opponent, the Jesuit school of Saint Ignatius. It was an open week on the schedule they had filled in to stay in shape. In an expected outcome, East Tech defeated the all-boys school 65–0 in a shortened game. Meanwhile, West Tech continued their undefeated streak as well.

## November 13 vs. Central

The following week, having defeated Saint Ignatius, all roads pointed to the Senate League championship being played between East Tech and West Tech. During the days before the game, Willaman kept his team healthy by mostly working on signal drills and place-kicking.

Their focus was on Toledo and West Tech the last two weeks of the season. As a mere formality, East Tech defeated Central 59–0.

## November 20 vs. Scott

The third week of November marked East Tech's biggest game of the season to date. It was their turn against Toledo's Scott High—the midwestern champs who had not lost a game in nearly three years. Scott had also tied for the national championship 7–7 the year before. It was lining up as East Tech's toughest challenge and would determine whether their game against West Tech the following week would be for both the local Senate League title and the Midwest title. By defeating both their Senate League rival West Tech and the defending Midwest champions Toledo, East Tech would have a chance at the national spotlight.

Willaman and the coaches suited up to play against the first string in a scrimmage during the week before the Scott High game. During one particularly hard practice, Berkowitz injured his foot, making him questionable for the game. On the last day of practice, Willaman decided to rest the team. He gathered them in the school gym, and going down the line from Jack to Johnny and the rest of the starters, he went over the expectations of each individual player. He outlined two strategies for the game, one if the weather cooperated and the other if the field was wet.

Because they were outsized by the burly Toledo players, they didn't want to play straight toward the opposing line. Instead Willaman preferred an open-field strategy like Ohio State used, allowing each player to beat his own man. A day with clear weather would be perfect for their strategy. If the rain came, however, they would have to play up close and huddled against Toledo, shifting the advantage to the heavier team.

The morning of the game, 500 East Tech fans rode more than 100 miles along the Lake Shore Electric Railway in five dedicated cars. Prominent members of the Cleveland community began wishing Willaman luck and letting it be known that should their boys win, they might be taking Toledo's place as No. 1 contender for the national crown.

In front of 10,000 fans, the light but speedy East Tech team scored an early touchdown in the first quarter. With the ball on their own 20-yard line, it looked like Scott would be the first team to make it to East Tech's end zone. Then suddenly Carlson intercepted the ball and tucked it under his arm. The East Tech team spread out, making perfectly timed blocks and allowing the big Swede to run 80 yards for the TD. It was the first time a team had reached Scott's goalposts.

For the remainder of the game, Scott continued their attack. The East Tech defense struggled somewhat, but Jack would still earn praise in the December 11, 1920, *Cleveland Gazette* as one of Cleveland's all-time linemen for stopping Toledo's forwards again and again. On defense he broke through the opposing line and tackled their backs for considerable losses. On offense he plowed through the defense, opening up holes for his own backs.

Yet despite Jack's performance, he was only one player, and the game was still neck and neck. The defending midwestern champs spent most of the game in East Tech's territory but could not convert. At one point, Scott brought the pigskin to the 1-yard line, but East Tech kept them from scoring on the drive. Toward the end of the fourth quarter, Scott continued its march downfield. This time, with only a few yards to go, they threw a pass into East Tech's end zone for a touchdown.

With the score tied in the final quarter, East Tech received the ball. The team tried for a pass down the sideline but fumbled the ball and lost significant yardage. An offside penalty then cost them 15 yards. As the minutes of the final quarter ticked off, East Tech found themselves with the game tied and the ball on their own 5-yard line. A short pass brought them 15 yards. Then on the next play, with one minute left, Berkowitz heaved the ball high into the air. Jack kept his man at bay. The ball sailed toward the center of the field. As it came down, it bounced from East Tech to Scott, tumbling in the air. It continued traveling toward Norty Behm, who grabbed it, turned, and with no one behind him, ran the remaining 60 yards to score the game-winning touchdown. East Tech squeaked out the victory 14–7.

### November 27 vs. West Tech

Having defeated the midwestern champions, all that was left for East Tech was to defeat West Tech to win both the Senate League and Midwest regional titles. Both East and West Tech were considered nearly unbeatable by the press and both had kept their league opponents from scoring on them the entire season. Berkowitz, still hurt, hadn't returned to practice. However, he was still expected to play in the West Tech game.

The day of the Senate League title game, the temperature was in the mid-30s and a slight mist of rain and snow wafted across the field. For the entire first half the two teams battled back and forth, unable to reach each other's end zones. Tough defenses and interceptions sucked the air out of the fans in the stands. The sound of the referee's whistle ended the first half with the score 0–0.

The second half, however, started with a bang. West Tech kicked off the ball as the crowd resumed its exuberant cries. The East Tech team lined up on the next play. Johnny received the ball into his hands and began to crisscross behind Jack and the other blockers, who were spreading out across the field. He flitted back and forth across the field, running a total of 57 yards to break the game wide-open with a touchdown. The East Tech fans roared their approval. West Tech tried to answer, but East Tech kept them out of their territory.

The droning cheers of 10,000 fans continued through the final quarter. Carlson, Berkowitz, and [first name unknown] McFadden each made a first down. Despite this, the Carpenters were unable to get into the end zone on the next three plays and were forced to punt the ball, giving their opponents a chance at tying the game. West Tech received the ball and made back-to-back first downs. Jack and the rest of the line pushed back with all their might, battling each man at midfield. The crowd watched the seconds of the clock tick down. Finally, with the ball lying on the East Tech 40-yard line, the referee blew the whistle, signaling the end of the game and East Tech's coronation as Cleveland's—and the Midwest's—champion.

Further accolades followed, cementing the star status of Jack and his teammates. As reported in the *Cleveland Gazette* on December 11, 1920, Cleveland's *News-Leader* and *Plain Dealer* dubbed the team both All-Scholastic and All-Senate football honorees. But what was next for the boys of East 55th Street? They had beaten Toledo, who had shared the previous year's national championship with the working-class town of Everett, Washington. Like his father before him, Jack's destiny called to him from the West.

# 3

# Baggy's Boys
# of Everett, Washington

EVERETT HIGH SCHOOL'S QUARTERBACK, GLENN "SCOOP" CARLSON, looked down at his relatively new football cleats. As one of Baggy's Boys, he and his teammates ruled high school football in the western United States. Now their uniforms finally reflected their excellence. Thanks to Everett's 1919 national co-championship with Toledo the season before, all the boys on the team were given new shoes. Up until then, the players had needed to supply their own equipment, including shoes, headgear, and pads. The families of Everett were working-class, often with several mouths to feed. Mothers took to sewing jerseys and leather headgear. Football cleats were expensive, so many of the boys resorted to wearing regular high-top shoes. There was a local cobbler who could fasten cleats to the high-tops, which made them a little more functional, but it was still a "compliment to call them football shoes."

Everett was a peninsula city whose skyline was filled with smokestacks. It was known as "the Pittsburgh of the West," and some would have told you it was the lumber capital of the world. Most of its inhabitants were mill owners and mill workers. It was perhaps one of the earliest blue-collar football towns. Standing in contrast to the burgeoning urban center of Cleveland, longtime Everett historian Larry O'Donnell described Everett as a "rough, tough, and raw town." It was a "perfect match" for the game of football.

The town's football dynasty began in 1910, the year after Welshman Enoch Bagshaw first came to the small city. He had been known for his play at the University of Washington, where he became captain and was credited with the school's first forward pass. After his college football career ended, his former teammate and center Pete Tegtmeier enticed him to join the faculty of Everett High School, where he could teach science, and more important, he could coach his own high school team.

Bagshaw and Everett's success grew, and along with it came a local interest in high school football. It trickled all the way down to grade schoolers and their parents, inspiring the townspeople to aspire to the ranks of Baggy's Boys, a familial legacy that often lasted for generations. In a small town of factories and mills, football became a point of pride, especially when the school played teams from nearby (but much larger) Seattle—and regularly won. As the population of Seattle increased, so did the number of its high schools. Eventually the metropolitan city could field its own league and didn't need to make the trip to Everett to fill their schedule, but if you asked the Everett locals, it was because they were afraid to lose again.

Initially the Everett team played on a local baseball diamond, but as football became a more serious business, Bagshaw got his own field. It was named Athletic Field, but it was known as Bagshaw Field, and the stands themselves were designed and built by the hands of the high school students. Bagshaw quickly became a polarizing figure, even among his own players. He ruled his fiefdom with a combination of innovative plays and rigorous discipline. Off the field he was Baggy, but on the field he was Coach Bagshaw.

To Scoop, however, there was a major flaw in how the team was run. Bagshaw personalized things too much. The young Swede also didn't take kindly to the coach's profanity on the field. Especially since it wasn't something he heard back inside his own conservative home. The unlucky folks who happened to live near the football field took to closing their doors and windows after school so as to be spared hearing one of Bagshaw's tirades. Sometimes the anger inside Scoop would boil so strongly, "it'd make you so mad you'd fight your own grandmother."

It quickly became no secret that the starting quarterback and his strong-willed coach didn't take too kindly to each other. Scoop wasn't alone in his feelings. Bagshaw made the mistake of scrimmaging with the team one time. A few of the older players made sure he never did that again. Scoop later summed up his personal conflict with Bagshaw as "a bull-headed Swede and a bull-headed Welshman." But Scoop also knew his coach's worth. He saw the coach as someone who played a poker game, and this guy was dealt a pretty good hand.

And in the end, they had the same mission: to win. Football was a game of attrition. In those days, if you were substituted out during the first half of the game, the rules stated you couldn't return until the next half. If the substitution happened in the second half, you were out of the game for good. Bagshaw focused on making stamina an advantage. Practices would last for hours. When it became too dark to see the other players, Bagshaw would move the team under the streetlights. Once practice was over, Bagshaw would call out, "Three times around the track, fellas!" Followed by a pause, a narrowing of his eyes, and then, "Five times for you, Carlson." The Welshman ran around the inside of the track to make sure the young quarterback didn't cut any corners. It was another five blocks uphill from the running track to the high school. Because Scoop had to run two extra laps, by the time he made it to the locker room, all the hot water would be gone. The remaining cold water merely bounced off "the grim and the grime" coating his body, leaving him to walk home cold and caked with dirt.

"Superb physical condition" was the goal. At the time, the rulebook called for four 15-minute quarters. Many high school coaches would agree before their games that 15 minutes was too long and would instead use 12-minute quarters for high school kids. Bagshaw wouldn't hear of it and scoffed at the notion. He knew his team, and most of them wouldn't even break a sweat with 15-minute quarters. Substitutions and 48-minute games were for the weak.

Scoop knew this too. Players were expected to shake off any injuries. And as the quarterback, after each play he was expected to be the first one up. As soon as he pulled himself off the ground, he would scan to see if any of his teammates were injured. Better he saw someone hanging his head and catching his breath than Bagshaw, because if the coach saw it, the player would be pulled from the game. Scoop would often go to his best ball-handler if he was down and pull him up to save the guy's energy. If anybody looked slow regrouping, he knew not to give him the ball. The same was true on the other side of the ball. If it looked like someone on the defense was struggling, holding his arm, or limping, that's where Scoop would direct his attack.

He also knew that despite his personal differences with Bagshaw, the team represented something bigger than itself. It was the sinews that held the city together, even as it tried to pull itself apart. Everett was a city "at war with itself." It was a prosperous town, but one that knew the difference between the haves and the have-nots. It still bore the scar of 1916, when a steamship carrying workers from the Industrial Workers of the World (IWW) Union from Seattle arrived at the Everett docks. It was a time of palpable tension between union workers and business owners. The local sheriff had deputized nearly 200 people who waited for the workers to arrive, fearing they were there to start protests. Many of them waited on the docks and on a tugboat, armed and ready. When the union leaders attempted to disembark, a confrontation with the sheriff quickly escalated and shots rang out. Several people were killed and many more were injured. It was known as the Everett Massacre, and the wound it opened—especially concerning labor relations—stayed tender to the touch.

The only thing that seemed consistent was Bagshaw and high school football. From 1911 to 1919, the team had only lost one game to another high school. They played some varsity college teams during that stretch for the learning experience. The team's success became a source of comfort and of common ground to a town trying to heal. Outscoring opponents by 10 times on average gave the community the much-needed feeling of success, and of relative importance. According to the *Everett Daily's* Nels "Rosy" Weborg, "It did not matter whether it was a banker or laborer, merchant or professional man. They all met on common ground when Baggy and football were under discussion. The rich man would discuss it by the hour with his poorest neighbor."

Before the 1920 season even began, while Jack was back home in Hiram, Bagshaw had begun his constant promotion of his team in Washington. He wasted no time sending out telegrams to Seattle, Tacoma, and Spokane in an effort to secure a Northwest Championship Game for his boys. Eugene, Oregon, had already declined, citing its inability to provide Everett the level of competition it sought. Wenatchee, Washington—despite having a back nicknamed Hippo because of his size—gracefully declined. Whitman College in Walla Walla, Washington, also joined the growing list of schools choosing to keep their pride, and their men, intact. Other teams, such as that in Chehalis, Washington, initially accepted but then backed out, citing concerns with Everett's player eligibility and sportsmanship.

The unstoppable Everett team not only ran out of high school teams in its own state to play against, it ran out of high school teams *period.* In just its second game of the 1920 season, Everett squared off against the Navy team from Navy Yard Puget Sound in Bremerton, Washington. They boasted a team full of high school graduates and some college football graduates. Size and experience were clearly on their side, as was their military-level physical fitness. The Navy squad weighed at least seven pounds more per person than the Everett team. Their commanding officer recommended that they not get too rough with the young boys. They lost 27–9 to the high schoolers, with four of the touchdowns scored against them in the last six minutes of the game. The next week, Everett beat the Naval Base Hospital team, another older military team, 84–0.

With a break in the schedule, Bagshaw organized a road trip for the boys to watch the University of Washington freshman football team take on Saint Martin's College. The game ended in a 0–0 tie. While the game may have seemed like a bye-week diversion, Bagshaw, ever focused on making his team the best, was there on a scouting mission. He had already pulled some strings and arranged for his own team to play both of the collegiate-level teams during the next two weeks. Everett left the games against both collegiate teams without giving up a single point.

On November 11, 1920, the town of Everett waited for the next chapter in their football history to unfold. It was Armistice Day, the annual celebration of the 1918 armistice agreement signed between the Allies and Germany, signaling the end of fighting in World War I. A local parade of torches, cars, and floats lit up the night as it snaked its way out from the high school. A large bonfire also attracted crowds of revelers. The town eagerly awaited the arrival of a team from The Dalles in Oregon. Having defeated all the Washington State challengers, Everett had broadened its sights to nearby Oregon. There, The Dalles had finished their season undefeated in their own state. The team represented a major stepping-stone toward the elusive national championship, and Bagshaw was eager to bring them to his home turf. Ticket prices were raised to 50 cents for students and a full dollar for adults to cover the expense of bringing their opponents to the hometown field.

The game began in front of a record crowd, a heavy wind blowing across the field. Everett kicked off, and almost immediately after the first play, they forced a fumble by The Dalles. Everett recovered the ball on the 32-yard line and promptly marched down the field to score their first touchdown. The Dalles got the ball back on the next kickoff but were forced to punt. On the next series, Everett was held at bay, but when they punted, the heavy wind took the ball out of bounds. This gave the visitors from Oregon the opening they needed and allowed them to score a game-tying touchdown.

Everett responded to the touchdown and the wind by keeping the ball on the ground and calling steady running plays. A series of short runs set them up for a second touchdown, and they regained the lead. The momentum began to shift in front of the boisterous and hardened hometown crowd. The Dalles were stopped once more and Everett recorded a third touchdown to end the first quarter. From then on, it was Everett's game as the Oregon state champions were scoreless in the next three quarters. The final scoreboard read Everett 90, Dalles 7.

Two weeks later, the best high school team in Utah—East High School, which had won the state championship for three years in a row—came to try their hand at Everett, captained by the best quarterback in their state. Bagshaw invited both the University of Washington president and its football team as guests and witnesses to the feat. He also invited the coach of Dartmouth to the game, but it was still unclear if he would make it there from back east. The nearby streets were closed to cars and other machines to make room for the expected fans and subsequent celebration.

Wet grass coated the cleats of the Everett team as it squared off against East High School. Heavy rains the night before had left their mark on the gridiron. Crowds arrived early, filling the additional bleachers erected for the game. Shortly before noon, the sun came out and bounced between the stands and the field. First the visitors and then the hometown team came out to successively louder cheers and began their warm-ups on separate ends. Utah passed the ball back and forth while Everett practiced calling and executing snap plays down its half of the field.

Both teams started the game nervous about their opponents and the slippery conditions. Everett started with the ball and executed a series of runs but fumbled for a turnover. Recovering their composure, they kept the pressure on their opponents, forcing them to punt. Everett got back into its groove, running the ball downfield for an eventual touchdown. The rest of the quarter saw Everett repeatedly attacking their opponent's end zone, but the real star of the first 15 minutes was a seagull that hovered less than 10 feet above the players. It circled the field three or four times, drawing cheers from the fans below. Some spoke of the bird as a good omen of things to come, for it had been seen during the previous game too. Those prognostications were on target, as the game saw Everett win 67–0 against the three-year Utah state champions.

The victories over Oregon and Utah gave Bagshaw the ammunition he needed to secure a championship game in California. By beating the western states, he would then be able to challenge a team east of the Mississippi River, and Everett could claim its rightful spot as the undisputed national high school champion. In the Golden State, Long Beach Polytechnic Institute had won a rigidly tiered high school football system, ensuring only the best of the best made it out on top. The team's storied past involved wins over Nevada, Arizona, and New Mexico. In three years, it had outscored its opponents 1,108–34. In 1920 alone, it had scored 438 points to its opponents' 7, with the sole touchdown against them resulting from an unlucky fumble that was returned into the end zone. If Everett managed a victory over Long Beach, Bagshaw eyed a New Year's Day event touted as the National High School Championship Game. He would reserve naming their opponent until his team officially secured the win in California.

Bagshaw and the local boosters arranged for a private train car to take the team from Seattle to Los Angeles. It would serve as the local headquarters for the team in enemy territory. Bagshaw also requested large 10-gallon milk jugs to be filled with water from Everett and transported with the team to the game, as he didn't trust the California water. The team would also be accompanied by a local Everett reporter, who would provide constant telegraphs back home on the "comings, goings, and doings" of the historic team.

The night they left for Seattle, the team was invited for a local banquet. The master of ceremonies was local newspaper columnist Rosy Weborg, who thanked Bagshaw for "developing real he-men." Bagshaw, in turn, presented a golden football to the local doctors primarily responsible for helping patch up the team after "the rough usage handed the boys" in their "hard contests." Bob Abel, a former quarterback for the team, was also one of the speakers. He vented his frustrations regarding rumors that had been circulating about Everett regarding ringers and cheating. "Those wild statements are rotten deals," he declared. "Everett has been criticized because she has won."

Through wind and rain, the team's train car made its way down south. At each stop—and there were many of them—the boys would get off the train to throw the football around, or if time and weather permitted, run up and back to the local town. On the train, the usual ribbing of teammates covered such things as who looked like they had never set foot outside their small town or whether a certain player was sleeping in the hammock reserved for clothes instead of the actual bed—a reference to their level of intelligence.

Another player came across an orange grove for the first time, and with the owner's permission, he chose two perfect specimens. His "treasure" seemed less impressive to his teammates. The team collected makeshift ribbons, balloons, and pennants along the way and adorned the team car with them. The word EVERETT was emblazoned on the outside of the team car, the result of a local depot store chalk purchase.

As the team neared the end of its four-day journey, floods and a landslide marked their entrance into California. Scoop sauntered outside the car to see what the hold-up was and saw a team of workers clearing rocks and debris off the track. Fearing they were taking too long, he rushed back to the car and suggested the team get out and help. "Great training stuff," he remarked. After a quick debate, the boys' understanding and interpretation of local union rules dictated that they were better off staying in the comfort of their beds than otherwise helping with the arduous labor. Once the tracks were passable, the train passed through the "fruit belt" of Fresno and the oil fields of Bakersfield. A stop in the desert allowed for a quick gathering of souvenir cacti. Still in high spirits, the boys finally made their way into the City of Angels, their faces pressed up to the windows of the train as they spotted "wild" palm trees for the first time.

The morning of the game, Everett was bustling with anticipation; the townspeople had sent 50 to 60 telegrams to the team wishing them the best. A dedicated telegraph wire had been established between California and Everett so that the play-by-play could be sent to the local Rotary Club. Every bulletin would be read and each play would be marked by a giant football board displayed in the local Rose Theater. Classes would be let out so the students could watch a similar six-foot-by-eight-foot board in the school auditorium. The dress code of the day had been declared "loud tie and pig-tails," and the student body boldly complied. Everyone's eyes were on the clock, waiting for the time the whistle would blow in Long Beach. Finally the time for the game arrived. A slight delay in getting the Rose Theater board system up and running was punctuated with excited cheers when finally the little red and blue lights lit up and blinked along its edges. The local Boy Scouts band struck up a song to celebrate.

Back in California, the 15,000 fans present at the game eagerly hummed in excitement. A nervous Scoop stood at the helm of his team. He had heard how much bigger the California team was, and up close, the rumors proved true. His teammates on the ends listened to the opposing players and fans chuckling at Everett's shoddy-looking uniforms, which only served to inspire the mill workers' sons. As Scoop lined up for the first play of the game, he felt alone on the field. During the first series of downs, Everett made no progress against the Long Beach team. Both teams, however, failed to get into a groove as Long Beach fumbled and Everett was intercepted. Bagshaw and Everett called a timeout. The discussion lasted long enough that they were penalized for a delay of game, but the message was received. Their nerves began to steady, and Everett lined back up.

Out of the corner of his eye, the local Everett reporter spotted something hovering above the field. He turned to see a seagull flying over the end of the field. He quickly ran to the telegraph operator. The message ran over the wire and was read out loud to the crowds in the

Rose Theater and school auditorium: "A large white seagull is flying over the corner of the field." The town erupted in cheers. Their symbol of impending victory had arrived.

It didn't take long for Scoop and the rest of the team to see something beginning to break in the Californians. Scoop could see they weren't in the same shape as Baggy's Boys were. It was only a matter of time before they began to run out of fuel and fall back to Earth like all the others before them. First their lungs failed and then their minds. The next series saw Everett score its first touchdown, followed by back-to-back fumbles by Long Beach. The beginning of the second quarter arrived along with a third Everett touchdown.

The second half proved no easier for Long Beach. If they tried attacking by air, the ball was intercepted. By ground, they fumbled. The Long Beach team was noticeably weaker by the end of the third quarter, having been pushed to their limit by the grit and determination of Everett's line. The fourth quarter unfolded with yet a fourth Everett touchdown. A final effort by the California team saw them reach Everett's 3-yard line, only to be stopped dead in their tracks. Three straight attempts to score were swallowed up by the Everett defense. As the referee began to blow the final game whistle, the crowd joined the players on the field in celebration. Long Beach's coach, stunned by the loss, had been eyeing a game against Chicago for the national spotlight. Those hopes vanished, as the game was immediately called off. It no longer had any significance. Any request for his comment by the press was met with silence as he left the field with his exhausted players in tow. Bagshaw, on the other hand, saw his mythical national championship nearly materialized. With the taste of victory still on his lips, he declared that on New Year's Day, Everett would play against the best team the rest of America had to offer.

# 4

# A Call to the West

JACK AND HIS TEAM WERE STANDING PROUDLY ONSTAGE IN THE SCHOOL auditorium when the news came across the telegraph. Jack stood onstage as somewhat of a local celebrity. His reputation had been growing within Cleveland's African American community. He joined a rare few who were publicly honored on and off the field. Yet it was a tenuous position to hold. The *Advocate*, Cleveland's local Black newspaper, warned that when Black athletes were honored, they also became targets. As a result, the paper argued, they must "assimilate more ability, more stamina, more spirit, more nerve, and more generalship" than their White counterparts to overcome the obstacles placed in front of them. But the paper also stated that "it is in athletics that we are permitted to be recognized."

This recognition, the *Advocate* argued, should not be manifested through people reading about the athlete in the newspaper at home. But instead the athlete should be inspired in person by being cheered from the sideline. The paper implored its readers not to sit back, not to wait until the athlete had accomplished all he could and then stand up and offer their hand in congratulations. No, the paper encouraged readers to be at the game to cheer for him. For what was the value of having him look around only to be cheered by Caucasian faces? It became the responsibility of those around the athlete and in his community to lend "aid that [would] make a new luminary in the slowly rising horizon of equality."

It was during the morning assembly when the news reached the school. The East Tech football team was receiving their varsity sweaters and letters when things suddenly came to a stop. The *Plain Dealer* had wired Bagshaw for a definitive answer, and his response had just come over the wire. The contract was official. Everett was inviting East Tech to their hometown to play for the national high school championship. Not only that, but to help defray part of their travel expenses and ensure they made it, Everett would also be wiring $5,000 to them.

The pep rally intensified. Players and students began murmuring excitedly over the sound of the school band. The coaches consulted railway maps and guides, and travel plans were quickly patched together. The team would take the train west the next day toward Los Angeles, and then up the Pacific coast to Seattle, where Everett would be waiting for them.

BY THE TIME the news reached Willaman and his boys in Cleveland, the Everett team had already arrived back home in Washington from Los Angeles. Upon arriving home, the team was met at the station by a 50-piece band. The crowd surged forward in waves under the tinsel and trees of a small-town Christmas. The police on the platform did their best to get the boys through the throngs of people eager to get a look at their victors. They were paraded into town on the wings of an automobile caravan. The celebration climaxed at the Rose Theater, where the team and hundreds of fans were shown the film of the Long Beach game. Most of them had only seen it played out on the electric board a few days earlier. Additional showings were scheduled for Christmas Eve and twice on Christmas Day. After all, what better present from Santa, they said, than witnessing Baggy's Boys bring home the bacon on the big screen? The film, it was noted, really showed how big those boys down in California were. And boy, how they fell!

There was planning to do. The local Elks Lodge had already wrapped up a rousing meeting where committees were made and plans were enacted to double the seating capacity of Athletic Field from 5,000 to 10,000. Tiers upon tiers of bleachers were called for—under careful guidance of local engineers, of course. Ultimately they wanted a complete stadium effect to complement the steep increase in ticket prices. Tickets would be sold at Brewster's and Owl Drug Store. To keep up with demand, someone was expected to be stationed at Owl around the clock. Tickets were to be sold to the hometown crowd first before sales were opened up to the surrounding communities. This, after all, was Everett's team!

THE CARPENTERS WOULD leave Cleveland's Union Depot for their six-day journey at 8:00 AM the morning of Christmas Eve. Their plan was to make it to Los Angeles, where they would have a seven-hour stop. During that time, they would get in a quick workout and also rendezvous with Coach Willaman's brother Frank, who was playing for Ohio State. The Buckeyes would be in California that weekend in advance of playing the California Golden Bears in the Rose Bowl on January 1, 1921. The East Tech team would then arrive in Seattle on December 30, where they would have two days of practice on the University of Washington's field before facing off on New Year's Day.

According to the papers, Everett's boys outweighed East Tech's by an average of 20 pounds. Willaman assured everyone those numbers were wrong and made sure to list his players as a bit heavier when the next round of newswires came out. Yet he still knew, now more than ever, that his boys would need to rely on their Ohio State–style aerial game. They would need Berkowitz's arm, the Behm brothers' speed, and Jack's strong tackling if they were to have a chance.

On the morning of their departure, the train pulled away from the station with a surge, leaving behind 2,000 cheering East Tech fans. The train traveled two days until it reached Omaha. During that time Johnny and Jack spent time talking to each other. While stuck on the train, eating was a highlight of their day, and Johnny would often follow Jack to the dining car, where the Black porters often winked and snuck Jack some extra food. When they weren't eating or talking, the boys would gaze out at the changing landscape. Far from the factory lights of Cleveland, they were suddenly surrounded by nighttime skies filled with twinkling stars. Their days were marked by the tall silhouettes of silos against backdrops of grain.

Christmas on the train was marked with carols and fruit baskets that the girls of East Tech had given the boys before they left Cleveland. One of the most memorable highlights, however, was the discovery of a stowaway. A local high school freshman had boarded the train with the team only to be discovered by the coaches. His pleas and enthusiasm fell on deaf ears as he was left on the platform at the next station after the players had scrounged some money together to buy a return ticket for the lost soul.

As the team came and left Omaha, ticket sales had opened up in Everett. Long lines of people waited for their chance to see their hometown heroes in action. Brewster's had run out of tickets to sell, and frantic calls were being made to get more tickets over to them as soon as possible. Meanwhile the official ticket headquarters at Owl Drug Store was similarly overwhelmed. The hottest ticket seemed to be in the new grandstands, which were actively being built at the same time the ticket money was changing hands. Within an hour of opening sales, the grandstand level was sold out. The demand remained so high that scalpers began to pop up and began to work their way through the crowds in line.

By the second day of sales, half the tickets were already gone. Spalding sporting goods store in Seattle called in to Owl insistently asking for a chance to sell a batch of tickets to its customers. Bagshaw began running his first practice since Long Beach. He had a good idea that East Tech was better than Toledo, a team his team had tied 7–7 only one year earlier. He still had much of the same team, which meant it would likely be the hardest high school game they played under his watch. He also didn't have to worry about any teams from the East Coast trying to lay claim to the title. West Tech had beaten one of the best teams New England had to offer, and East Tech had bested both them and Toledo. The Carpenters were being called the best team east of the Rockies. Things were finally coming together, he thought, for a true national championship.

WITH JUST TWO days to go until the big game, the East Tech team arrived in Los Angeles for a short layover. To keep in shape, they took a three-mile jog with Willaman sitting comfortably in the van barking at them. Then they took a quick rest while they drove the short distance to Pasadena where Willaman's brother and Ohio State were getting ready for the Rose Bowl. The two championship contenders mingled and practiced together. Each East Tech boy undoubtedly imagined himself on the university football field playing for a college championship someday.

For Jack it was a distant idea but not completely far-fetched. A handful of Black players had found spots on professional football teams in the Ohio State League, and several others had made headlines playing for college teams. It was still a rarity, but if he gave his life over to it, football could be a ticket to a different future.

After the quick turnaround in Southern California, the East Tech squad made its final transfer in Portland and arrived in Seattle on December 30 as planned. They made themselves home at the New Washington Hotel, the city's premier 14-story hotel. They were welcomed by the same marble hotel lobby that had greeted presidents and later would see Elvis Presley. In less than 48 hours, the new year would be upon them, bringing with it an exciting possibility of becoming the country's top high school football team.

THE SHOWDOWN WAS set for high noon. It was New Year's Day 1921, a Saturday. Most businesses were closed, making the high school championship a perfect occasion to ring in the new year. Jack and his team woke up early on New Year's Day in their luxury hotel rooms. They ate breakfast with a nervous quiet among them. Everyone grabbed their gear and headed to the local football field for a quick workout. Willaman went over some final plans and preparations before the team traveled the 30 miles to Everett.

A wave of nervousness and excitement washed over the town. East Tech arrived at Everett High School at 9:30 AM and were escorted to the locker room. The gates to the field opened at 10:00 AM, by which time large crowds had already gathered. The fans began to file into the stands, where ushers directed them to their seats. They had strict instructions to be seated by the time the referee blew his whistle at 12:00. The top tiers were filled first, so that all 8,000 fans could be packed into the bleachers. Like a symphony or play, instructions were sent out that anyone who arrived late would have to wait for a timeout or the end of a quarter to be seated. Large swathes of the street were roped off from automobiles. Where cars were allowed to park, a new method of parking was being tried that was apparently "in vogue in Tacoma." The cars were backed in with their wheels to the curb and their radiators facing outward so they would not have to back into traffic upon leaving. On one side of the sprawling field, 600 members of the Elks Lodge mingled, clad in purple and white and surrounding their fully uniformed band. A large stuffed elk loomed over them. Banners were scattered across the newly erected stands, which visibly shook but did not yield.

The sky was overcast but not rainy. A light drizzle had given the air a crispness, and a light breeze wafted from the south. The town itself seemed quiet beyond the borders of the field and the roads leading to it. Signs in hotel windows announced, ALL ROOMS TAKEN. Several townspeople hurried about their business to the few shops that were still open, but not being football fans, they had very little to say. All but two or three cafés had taped papers on their doors announcing they were closing by 11:30 for the big game. With the exception of a few stragglers mingling from the previous night's New Year's Eve masquerade ball, even the cigar store and pool hall remained somewhat desolate.

At the entrance to Athletic Field, students sold programs and postcards of Everett and its team. Food vendors were kept outside the stadium so as not to block anyone's view. A final wave of fans from Seattle arrived on buses and interurban trolleys. A long line of cars had made their way into town, forming a procession from the Pacific

Highway to Hewitt Avenue. On the sidewalk, one onlooker paused to look at his watch. As 60 seconds ticked by, he counted 47 cars, some carrying as many as 10 people, heading toward the stadium. Two large film cameras hovered on stands above the field. The stage and audience were set. At eight minutes before noon, both teams took the field, and Jack Trice became the first African American football player to walk onto Everett's grass.

The opening kickoff saw Berkowitz receive the ball and run it back to the 49-yard line. Everett held tightly for three plays, forcing a punt by East Tech. Big Swede Carlson kicked the ball in the air, and it was caught downfield by Scoop Carlson. Everett began its own attack, stringing a few runs together. Both teams appeared nervous on their opening drives and didn't make much headway. The crowd continued with its dull roar.

East Tech tried again to push through Everett's line but to no avail. The remainder of the first quarter saw a series of back-and-forth action with no real gains. Then, just as the initial adrenaline of the crowd started to wane, a small seagull appeared out of the clouds. It swooped down and circled the field. The band played and the crowd pointed. Everett's good luck omen had arrived. Feeling the energy of the crowd, Baggy's Boys dug in deeper and pushed the ball to East Tech's 2-yard line as the referee signaled the end of the first quarter.

As the teams lined back up to start the second quarter, the white bird returned for a second time, it's gentle arc forming a figure eight above the field. Just as the school's new official mascot ascended back into the clouds, Everett broke through East Tech's line to score the first touchdown of the game and the second touchdown all season against the team from Cleveland. The student section erupted in hugs and high-fives. The Elks patted each other on the back. Cheerleaders barked into large cardboard megaphones. And the crowd joined together in unison:

*Say?*

*What?*

*That's What?*

*What's What?*

*That's What We All Say!*

*What Do We All Say?*

*EVERETT-EVERETT-EVERETT!*

East Tech received the ball and started its own series of running plays. Behm and Swede Carlson took turns making some modest gains. Everett looked like it was starting to falter. Each time East Tech touched the ball, it took two or three Everett men to tackle the carrier. Nevertheless, East Tech was unable to convert and the ball went back to Everett. The two teams swapped scoreless series, neither one giving their opponent an inch.

*Rickety-Rick-Rack*

*Chickety-Chick-Chack*

*Give 'em the horse laugh*

*HAAAAWWWW*

East Tech caught the ball off an Everett punt, but Berkowitz fumbled it on the 10-yard line. The ball squirted out from under an Everett player and skittered across the goal line, where Berkowitz managed to jumped on it, only to be hurled back over the goal line by Everett's much larger lineman, giving a safety to the team from Washington. The scoreboard changed to 9–0.

*ROUSE 'EM EVERETT HIGH*

*SOUSE 'EM EVERETT HIGH*

*ROUSE 'EM, SOUSE 'EM, EVERETT HIGH!*

Back on defense, Everett intercepted a pass from East Tech and ran it to the 25-yard line. They lined up again and moved the ball to the left, where an opening led to the ball lying on East Tech's 3-yard line. Another play and another touchdown for Everett brought the score to 16–0. The Carpenters mounted a determined drive of their own from their 16-yard line to within 20 yards of Everett's end zone but were unable to get the touchdown they so desperately wanted. The half ended with an exhausted East Tech team marching off the field toward the benches. A few of them looked up to see the Everett crowd giving them a standing ovation for their effort. Disappointment gave way to a few smiles between Jack and his teammates.

As the crowd began to turn its adulation toward its own team, a small Black boy cautiously emerged from the crowd, shuffling along the edge of the field. Five-year-old William Davis had been lingering by the press box all day. In his hand, he clutched a chocolate bar to his chest and looked longingly across the field.

"What is it?" asked one of the veteran newspaper writers during the half.

"I want to give this present to *him*," responded the small child, pointing at Jack. "And I'm afraid they mightn't like it if I go out there," he said, indicating the field in front of him.

"Go ahead, little fellow. It's all right," the man in the press box assured him.

Without another word, the child ran across the field, stopped in front of Jack, and tossed his prized candy into the lineman's lap. His mission accomplished, he immediately turned back the way he had come and disappeared back into the crowd. Jack looked down and then up again at where the Black child had been standing on the grass. A visible tear formed in the corner of his eye. Johnny and the other players sitting next to Jack bit their own lips to hide their emotions.

During the rest of the halftime, the crowd excitedly talked about the score favoring Everett but also how tricky the East Tech backs were. They looked pretty dangerous in the open field, and every tackle that had been made by an Everett man saw him going headfirst and reaching out as far as he could to contain East Tech from breaking the game wide-open. It felt good to be winning, but Everett's toughest battle seemed to be living up to the hype. They felt as if they were trying to keep a rumbling volcano from exploding. The second half, they knew, would not be easy.

The third quarter began much as the first quarter had. Both teams were cautious not to give an inch. When a hole did open up, every man rushed to help close it up. As the quarter wore on, the crowd became more and more excited to watch East Tech show off its open-field play. Berkowitz let several big passes fly, and both Behm brothers and Swede showed an agility that delighted all but the most hard-core Everett fan. It was a show both sides enjoyed.

The third quarter ended without either team scoring, but some in the crowd began to murmur that East Tech was starting to turn the tide with its repeated forays into Everett's territory. The highlight of the game may have been Swede's fake punt and pass to Johnny Behm, who lost his leather helmet and ran the ball for 40 yards.

The fourth quarter started with East Tech stopping Everett deep in its own territory and forcing a punt to midfield. Berkowitz received the ball on the 45-yard line and, amid cheers from both ends of the field, returned the ball to the 25-yard line. Two plays later, Berkowitz threw the ball down the sideline to Johnny Behm, who turned and ran 20 yards into the end zone. Some in the crowd thought this was the beginning of a come-from-behind victory for East Tech.

A fierce battle was waged for what remained of the fourth quarter, both teams reaching deep within themselves to run faster and tackle harder. Jack held the line for his team as it found its second wind. Everett, which had scored almost at will for two years, did not reach the end zone for the entire second half. The Washington team that rarely broke a sweat required a timeout to breathe with five minutes left. However, despite numerous aerial attempts, East Tech failed to capitalize. The clock ticked down before the Carpenters could score again. Jack watched as the referee brought the whistle to his lips and let out a final blow just as the jubilant crowd rushed onto the slightly muddy field. Those in the stands who couldn't make it down the stairs with their brethren threw their hats into the air. The final score was Everett 16, East Tech 7. Church bells rang across the city. Mills blew their whistles. Tugboats honked their horns in the harbor. Baggy and Everett finally won their mythical high school national championship. And Jack quietly became a little boy's hero.

THE CELEBRATION LASTED into the night. It only took six and a half minutes for the *Herald*'s presses to begin churning out newspapers claiming victory. Both teams had been invited to a dinner at Weiser's, the premier restaurant in Everett. There was also the opportunity for dancing at Redmen Hall after the dinner for the out-of-towners. Both teams attended the dinner. It was a collegial event for the boys and the coaches, where Willaman and Bagshaw took turns praising each other and their teams.

Jack, however, had another invitation. Everett didn't have any official rules related to segregation, but there was a clear separation of color when it came to social activities. Jack was provided an alternative where not only would he be among other people of color, he would also be the guest of honor. A dinner party was organized at the local home of the Samuels family. The Samuels name was well-known among the

African American families of Everett. The most visible members were Jennie and John Samuels, who lived on Hoyt Avenue in the Bayside area of Everett, mere blocks from Everett High School. The Samuels resided at that address for nearly 50 years, raising their son Wesley, whose deep voice, it was said, could make one weep with the sound of a sad song. The African American couple were prominent members of the minority community in Everett. Jennie was very active in the State Federation of Colored Women's Clubs. Their home would be included in the 75-cent *The Negro Motorist Green Book*, a travel guide that began publication in 1936 to provide safe destinations for journeying African Americans. The 1949 edition listed three entries for "Tourist Homes" in Everett. Outside of nearby Seattle, not a single restaurant was listed in the state of Washington.

The Samuels opened their doors to strangers and friends alike. And in 1921, following the high school national championship game, they opened their doors to Jack. Visitors staying at the house from nearby towns and as far away as Texas thanked Jack for his journey west and his honor on the gridiron. Following dinner, a rousing series of songs by the house's guests brought Jack's heart back home.

Later that evening, the Black residents of Everett, as well as their out-of-town guests, enjoyed their own dance celebration at the IOOF Hall. The IOOF—the Independent Order of Odd Fellows—was a two-century-old organization aiming to promote personal and social development in one's community. It was at their hall where Jack was brought onstage and presented a 1921 Everett High School pennant. Jack spoke to the largely Black crowd, thanking them for their generosity and remarking on his admiration of Everett's team and its people. He hoped to return with East Tech the following year to play again, but beyond that, he even hoped to return to the West Coast one day to live.

As both parties let out, the two groups merged at the train station like small organisms merging into something bigger than themselves. They continued their singing and celebration as a whole body. Jack rejoined his team, and they boarded the Great Northern Railway. The train departed the station and headed east, leaving the western limit of America behind it.

# 5

## Cora

WHILE JACK WAS BUILDING A NAME IN THE BURGEONING METROPOLIS of Cleveland, Cora Mae Starlard had been attending high school in Ravenna, about 13 miles southwest of Jack's hometown of Hiram. In July 1919, she found herself looking out from the rostrum of the small Congregational Church. The attention of the audience was largely captivated by the performer on the piano, but a few of the younger kids were murmuring about the upcoming Fourth of July parade. It was expected to be the largest yet for the county, with soldiers marching and riding professionally designed floats. There would be men from the Great War, the Spanish-American War, and even from what some called the "dark days of '68," referencing conflicts during Reconstruction.

From the end of the row, Cora glanced to her right, examining many of the faces of the other 19 graduating fellow Ravenna High School students. It was said that this was the most interesting and brightest class in recent memory. Breaking with tradition, the seniors had chosen to furnish the speakers and entertainers for the ceremony from among their own ranks. Cora once again scanned the audience for her family. Despite the large number of attendees, it was relatively easy to pick out her relations, as she was the only Black member of the graduating class.

She spotted her mother, Alberta, and her stepfather, Claude. Alberta was a private nurse, part of a small but determined profession for Black women since the Civil War. Their ranks bore the likes of Harriet Tubman and Sojourner Truth. Cora; Alberta; Cora's father, Sam; and Alberta's mother and aunt had moved to Ohio from the mountains of Colorado shortly before Alberta and Sam divorced. Cora didn't know much about her father but had heard he moved somewhere around St. Louis.

Then Cora's mother met Claude in nearby Youngstown. They soon married and Alberta took Claude's last name, but Cora kept her father's last name, Starlard. Claude was a longtime chauffeur, something relatively new during the first quarter of the 20$^{th}$ century. Black men had been slowly finding employment as automobile drivers, transitioning from being draymen, who delivered beer and other goods on flatbeds pulled by horses or mules. Claude worked for John Pew, a steel magnate who had factories in Youngstown and Ravenna. The Pews became successful enough to buy a house known as the Merts mansion in Youngstown. The Pews were big-city folks and often invited Cora and her father to their Youngstown home.

As she sat at her graduation, Cora listened to the class valedictorian, Albert D. Olin, discuss how far the country had come since the Great War. Education was becoming ever more important, with literacy rates rising above 90 percent, a fact that was especially useful in rapidly training large groups of young men for combat. He then turned his attention to the importance of educating the minority populations of America, such as immigrants, Native Americans, and African Americans. He posited that educating the "great Negro population of the South" was an obligation. Albert, who went by A.D., stated, "The Indians have been looked after as a nation, but until late years no provisions whatever have been made for educating the Negro. Now, however, they will be included in the great nationwide movement of the abolition of illiteracy."

Later in the ceremony, Ethel Goss got up from her seat near Cora and strode to the podium. Her speech was titled "The Future Status of Women," a topic that had a strong connection to their little Ohio town. The country was on the verge of allowing women—at least White women—the right to vote. (Jim Crow laws would make it more difficult for Black women to realize their dream until almost half a century later, in 1965.) The women's suffrage movement had been pushed forward by women such as Elizabeth Cady Stanton, Susan B. Anthony, and Carrie Chapman Catt. Local Ravenna resident Harriet Taylor Upton had brought several meetings to her hometown, including the first statewide meeting of the Ohio Women's Rights Association, held nearly 70 years earlier in 1853.

"Do you realize the swiftness with which life is changing?" Ethel rhetorically asked the audience. She went on to contrast the changing attitudes toward women over the last hundred years.

"The woman of that day was ashamed to have an appetite, ashamed to be healthy, ashamed to be sensible, and to know anything; ashamed to do anything except some hideous and useless fancy work," Ethel said. She continued, "The woman of today is a strong, healthy woman and athlete, proud of her appetite. She is more frank, looks life straight in the eye, and is more able on the whole to take care of herself."

The messages resounded with Cora in two ways: She was both Black and a woman. She was now expected to both weigh on the American conscience and achieve more than those of her gender before her. Like Jack, she would be expected to better herself and her race.

Ethel enumerated the new professions women were finding themselves in—doctors, lawyers, and mayors among them. Never again, she declared, would women be looked at as inferior. That was a hallmark of a civilized nation.

Cora watched and listened while the young and optimistic White girl concluded with her final thought of inspiration: "With all the opportunities open to the ambitious and active woman of today, no woman need marry as a last resort because there is no other way of making a living. For upon the women depend the nobility, the force, the power, the wisdom of the world to come."

That summer Cora set out on her journey to find a living wage. Ravenna had seen rapid growth and an influx of industry, especially textile mills. Cora found a job at the Annevar Mill, at one of the city's two wool mills.

The wool business was putting Ravenna on the map, and the sprawling, bold red-brick Annevar Dye House screamed it out. Emblazoned across the top were the words, THE CLEVELAND WORSTED MILLS CO. Flanking each corner of the façade was the message, LOOK AT THE CLOTH! The Annevar Mill was one of two sister factories specializing in producing and dying worsted wool. The Annevar Dye House stood on Lake Street, and the Redfern Mill lay along South Chestnut. Regular wool was simply yarn woven together, but when it was produced in perfectly parallel fashion without any space between the fibers, it became luxurious worsted wool.

The factory owners had chosen Ravenna as an important satellite location because of its clean lake-sourced water, which could be used for their dyeing and finishing operations. The small Ohio town also provided access to three major railroad lines connecting Cleveland, Pittsburgh, Akron, Youngstown, and Canton. The town even invested in the short-lived Ravenna Aerial Company with an airfield about two miles northwest of Ravenna. The company made commercial, passenger, and exhibition flights, and even ran a short-lived flying school in 1919.

Mill workers such as Cora passed their 12-hour shifts in the five-story "daylight factory," so named for the way daylight burst through its huge windows and sprayed across its interior. In any large worsted factory, one might find bales of wool from local farmers sorted and stacked near bales hailing from England or Argentina. Each region of the world bore its own unique style of wool, determined by the pattern of scales coating the threads. The wool fleece was cleaned and combed through the mouths of carding machines grinning with iron and steel teeth. Under the watchful eyes of Cora and her coworkers, it was then stretched across combing machines, traveling along cylinders of undulating sizes. The Annevar Mill like its sister, the Redfern Mill, utilized several dyeing houses, where amid rising fumes, workers used long poles to stir the wool in large vats until it was ready to be dried. Finally the wool would be woven into patterns. Young girls would circulate among the mechanical looms using their small fingers to tie any broken threads before they became woven into the final product. From there, the finished cloth would be transported to Cleveland and then on to the garment centers of America.

Cora worked with her aunt Sadie, who was just a few years older than her. The two of them were both young and single. They stood on the precipice of a women's independence movement but were still held back from their White sisters' progress by their race. Finding a spouse would provide an important financial bedrock on which to raise a family. Nevertheless, similarly young and single Black men were hard to come by in the small towns scattered across the deeper parts of the Western Reserve.

Among the women working the mills, Cora did notice one sympathetic Black face among the shift workers. The woman was a hard worker in her fifties who had recently moved to Ravenna to live near her sister Fanny. Her husband had died a few years ago in Hiram, but her son still visited. It was said he was a "crack football player." It didn't take long for Cora to befriend the recent transplant. Anna was her name, and her son Jack was home from school for the summer.

JACK RETURNED TO his mother's new home in Ravenna during the summer of 1921. Ravenna was just a few train stops away from his, so he would sometimes see her during the school year, but during the summer he could find work in the small town to help ease his mother's financial burden. Jack found work as a mechanic with the Portage County Highway Department. Like many places in America, Ravenna's population was growing, and with it, the number of automobile drivers increased as well. Just a decade earlier, Portage County had only 54 registered cars. By 1920 the number was nearly 3,400. Even the local game warden took to patrolling his land in a Ford Model T.

Jack gave most of his weekly wages to his mother but reserved a small amount for the possibility that he might attend college after East Tech. Although some schools still did not accept Black students, Case Western University in Cleveland had a well-known science department. Jack had learned a lot about farming and agriculture at East Tech, and he had heard stories about Black farmers in the South, where both his parents had grown up.

Someone like Jack could learn animal husbandry or agriculture and take his knowledge down South to help Black farmers. Football was fun, but he needed to think about his future, and a profession. Guys like Johnny Behm could go play at any college they wanted. Jack had fewer options. Still, Coach Willaman had told Jack about Duke Slater, another Black player with exceptional skill. Slater had been given an opportunity to play at the University of Iowa and was making a name for himself. It was said that he might even play in the newly formed American Professional Football Association. It was being run by the country's greatest athlete and someone with whom Coach Willaman used to play professional football: Jim Thorpe.

Jack spent some of his free time in Ravenna jogging around town to keep in shape. He also spent time hanging out with a few of the other young men of color in Ravenna—his cousin Charlie Bunch and his friends Herb and Thad Proctor. Charlie's father had also died when he was young, but not before creating several patents for button fasteners. Charlie had been raised by Jack's aunt Fannie and had graduated from Ravenna High School. Following in his own father's footsteps as an inventor, Charlie would go on to get an electrical engineering degree from Ohio State University and eventually work his way to living a comfortable life in Beverly Hills.

Herb and Thad's family on their mother's side had also immigrated to Ohio from the South. Their grandfather served as one of the few African American sergeant majors in the Civil War. The Proctors could trace their family lineage back to the first Black settlers in 1795 Vermont. The brothers' father was a farmer who eventually opened up a respected local Ravenna business, the East End Meat Market.

Herb had recently moved back to Ravenna with his young wife and two small children after trying his hand as a truck driver in Cleveland. Thad was a few years older than Herb and worked as a local auto mechanic. If you were Black and in Ravenna, chances were you knew the Proctors.

Ravenna and its surrounding towns had also begun establishing their own Black Baptist and Methodist churches. These churches welcomed Black community members within their walls for both prayer and social activity. It was among these interlocking circles of Black Ravenna that Jack and Cora's paths crossed on a fateful summer day.

The summers in Ravenna were marked by the annual Portage County Fair, a tradition that had been nearly continuous since before the Civil War. Children, teenagers, and adults flocked to the fairgrounds to see the latest in motorized equipment, such as tractors, or advances in home science, such as new plumbing. Daredevils on high-wires awed the crowds. Races of all things known to man—from ostrich-drawn chariots to new racing automobiles—took place on tracks. The 1921 fair provided a respite from the recent tragedies of a war and a pandemic. It also provided much-needed entertainment for the young teenagers of small Ohio towns.

North of Ravenna, on the way to Kent, Brady Lake provided a summer camp–like environment for those seeking outdoor excursions. The land around the lake sported a manmade beach, carnival rides, a carousel, a dance hall, a roller coaster, and—new for 1921—a roller-skating rink. Its primary clientele comprised the "better class," meaning those from the cities who now found themselves with a little more leisure time and a little more money to spend, thanks to the advent of mechanization.

The dance hall became a particularly popular spot. A couple visiting Brady Lake from nearby Akron danced so "violently" that the girl's bare leg became visible to all who watched. The lewdness of such a thing prompted the couple to be ejected from the dance hall. A scuffle ensued that quickly prompted the jailing of the male companion. The dance hall attracted several Black bands performing the latest jazz sound, including the highly popular Fletcher Henderson Orchestra. Henderson was well on his way to becoming one of the most prolific jazz arrangers in music history and would eventually bring Louis Armstrong to New York from Chicago, forever solidifying the City That Never Sleeps as the epicenter of American jazz. Another act on the stage at the Brady Lake dance hall was the Seven Musical Magpies, described as "Colored Comedians with banjos and piano."

As much as they might have wanted to visit the amusement park and theater to see the African American bands perform, Cora and Jack might not have felt very welcome. The early 1920s saw the beginnings of the gradual growth of the Ku Klux Klan in the local Ohio communities. Klan activity had become especially notable in nearby Kent, and to a lesser extent in Ravenna. The sight of burning crosses lighting up the dark hillside beyond the river became an all too regular scene. In 1923 several hundred Klan members from Kent and Ravenna, many of them hooded, presented a Bible and an American flag to the principal of Brady Lake's new K–8 school. The ceremony was performed beneath the crackling light of a 30-foot fiery cross. Following the event, a hot meal was served to all by "women friends of the Klan." In the October 18, 1923, *Kent Tribune*, the Klan took out a large ad to promote its last open-air meeting of the season. The Portage Kounty Klan Konklave, as it was labeled, promised a "monster parade" and "big feed." Each "knight and lady" attending were encouraged to bring at least one other Portage County resident with them for candidacy.

While the Harlem Renaissance was being birthed in New York, the rest of the country bore witness to the rise of the KKK. Having initially grown from the Southern fear of Black independence following the

Civil War, the Klan used the fear of a post–World War I specter of the unknown immigrant to hijack a yearning among some struggling communities for social conservatism. By the end of 1921, the Klan claimed more than a million members. Jack's grandmother had been owned by racists. Jack's father fled them. Now, Jack and Cora lived among them.

# 6

# No Second Chances

IN THE FALL OF 1921, JACK RETURNED TO CLEVELAND, READY FOR HIS senior year of high school football. He was bigger and stronger. The little boy smiling in the yearbook on the junior team had the same smile, but now that smile emanated from a honed, muscular machine, ready for the next level of competition. Much of the team returned after summer break, eager to fight for the national title. Champ, Swede, and the Behm brothers all looked to reprise their roles from the previous year's record-breaking run that had taken them all the way to the Pacific coast. Berkowitz had graduated and moved on to play at Ohio State, so Johnny was anointed to take over as quarterback and captain of the team.

The season unfolded in almost a predictable fashion. Each week brought a hard-fought but expected victory. With the roster filled by veterans, East Tech continued its dominance over its Senate League rivals. The Carpenters outscored their opponents 320–28. The only team that came close to defeating them was their old nemesis from Toledo, Scott High.

The 1921 rivalry game weighed even heavier on everyone, for once again it emerged as a rung on the ladder pointing upward toward the national spotlight. The team from Toledo arrived with its own truck carrying radio equipment for what was a unique wireless broadcast, via which the game would be heard as far as 100 miles away. The roar of the 13,000 football fans was so loud it was said to be heard all the way back in Toledo itself. Johnny had been out with a knee injury for two weeks but came back for the big game against Scott. Once again, the team from Toledo stood as gatekeepers between East Tech and another shot at a national championship. The local paper claimed Scott had managed to grow and outweighed the Carpenters by 35 pounds per man. It was billed as one of the best high school games the region had seen. East Tech scored their first touchdown off a trick "sleeper" play. Swede tossed the ball to Norty as the Scott players were dumbfounded and didn't know how to react.

Toledo managed to answer with a touchdown of their own in the third quarter, and most of the rest of the second half was a hard-fought 7–7 battle. Neither team eased off the gas for a second. In the closing minutes of the fourth quarter, the two teams lined up for a Scott kick. As the kicker's foot made contact with the ball, Jack and Champ broke through the line. They both reached up, and one of them managed to block the ball, although it wasn't clear whose hand hit the pigskin first. Norty scooped up the loose ball and ran 80 yards for the game-winning touchdown. Clevelanders were still talking about the game 15 years later. Some claimed it was the greatest high school football game they had ever seen.

Following Scott's failure to knock them off, East Tech's last game of the regular season saw the Carpenters close out with a game filled with highlight-reel moments. Johnny had an unparalleled game. He scored six touchdowns, even running his way around the referee, who had to dive out of bounds to avoid the oncoming rocket on wheels. Jack played a spectacular game also, with several notable "wallops." His blocking complemented Johnny's directional changes and bursts of speed. Jack even plowed through the line on offense for a touchdown of his own. Following the final Senate League game of the season, East Tech was still eagerly awaiting to hear back about regarding a return trip to the West Coast. The league champs were also in negotiations to play the following weekend with New Britain, Connecticut, as it was believed they were the best the East Coast had to offer.

The *Cleveland Plain Dealer* selected its annual All-Scholastic Team. Named as top student-athletes were Johnny, Norty, Swede, Champ, and Jack. The paper also chose its All–Senate League Football Team. Included on that elite roster were Jack, Johnny, and Champ. The paper said that by playing steady, aggressive football, combined with his size and speed, Jack had made the East Tech's right flank "practically impenetrable." All signs were pointing toward a repeat game between East Tech and Everett for the national high school championship. But for reasons unknown, Everett chose to end their season without a championship game. They had remained just as much a force to be reckoned with in the Western League as before but had lost Enoch Bagshaw to a coaching job at the University of Washington. Although they remained unbeaten, without much explanation their new coach chose not to entertain any offers for postseason play. Eager to play for a national title, East Tech turned their eyes south.

BRAZOS COUNTY WAS painted with the same brush that swept across all of 1920s Texas. The local Brazos River fed rich cotton-producing land. Like many of its Lone Star neighbors, the county had also seen a recent rise in oil prospectors. They had come to town in search of

Texas gold, bringing men and money with them. The end of the 19th century had heralded the arrival of the International–Great Northern Railroad in 1873, and 1903 saw the opening of one of Andrew Carnegie's libraries in Bryan, the county seat of Brazos County. Not far south, Texas A&M College had opened its doors in 1876. Bryan quickly became a destination for businessmen interested in cotton, grain, oil, and cattle.

As the population in Texas grew, so did the number of schools. And with the schools came sports. By 1920 Texas high school football had organized itself under the University of Texas at Austin's University Interscholastic League (UIL). This planted the seeds of *Friday Night Lights*–style high school football that would grow across the fertile state.

The first official Texas high school football state championship was played in 1921. It was a bit of a stuttering start, as Houston Heights and Cleburne played to a 0–0 tie and claimed equal rights to the title. The state was hungry for a clear victor, and in the fall of 1921, Bryan, Texas, was making a name for itself. No other high school in Texas had scored a single point against them. In fact, no team had come within 30 yards of their end zone. And only one high school team had managed to claim a first down. The local juggernaut became a source of celebration. From the Rotary Club to the Baptist church, the players were honored across the town.

Soon the local team began looking outward for a worthy opponent to test its mettle. Everett wasn't looking for an opponent, but East Tech in Cleveland was. An offer came across the wire to Coach Willaman. Bryan offered to bring East Tech to Texas for a national championship game. The two teams would play in front of a crowd at Texas A&M to see which was best.

In the first week of December, the Carpenters accepted the challenge. Ohio Team May Soon Come to Bryan! read the December 8, 1921, headline in Bryan's local paper, the *Eagle*. The article went on to declare the game would "draw the greatest crowd ever in attendance at a high school football contest in Texas." History was to be made. Another paper—the *Brenham Daily Banner-Press*—declared on December 9, 1921, "Never in the history of high school football below the Mason-Dixon line, has an intersectional high school football game of such a stature been staged."

Jack's star was continuing to rise. His reputation as a barrier breaker was growing. He was described as being "to East Tech what the famous Fritz Pollard was to Brown University." (Pollard and Bobby Marshall had become the first two African Americans to play in the NFL, in 1920. Pollard went on to become the first African American head coach in the league.) But it was at that same Mason-Dixon line that Jack's celebrated climb came to an abrupt halt.

That's when the telegram arrived asking if East Tech had any Black players. In Texas, and in many other Southern states, Black and White players didn't mix. Segregation and "separate but equal" institutions remained strong. The UIL did not permit membership to African American schools. Its membership was reserved only for "any public white school." As a result, the Prairie View Interscholastic League (PVIL) was established, along with its own history of Black Thursday Night Lights. So when Southern schools played football against Northern schools, they sent telegrams confirming there were no Black players on the teams from the north.

As the football season of 1921 was wrapping up, racial tensions were running high across Texas. A sharp rise in lynchings within its state borders had begun in 1920 and was still underway. The Tulsa Race Massacre in the summer of 1921 had occurred just over the state line in Oklahoma. On October 11 of that year, 19-year-old Wylie McNeeley—who was the same age as Jack—was seized by a mob and burned alive at the stake. Nearly 1,000 people watched him die. A month and a half later, on November 30, 1921, Robert Murtore—a 15-year-old Black boy—was forcibly removed from police custody and shot in broad daylight. Less that two weeks later, on December 11, 55-year-old Fred Rouse was beaten, stomped, and stabbed in Fort Worth. Then he was abducted from his own county hospital bed, shot, and hanged from a tree. Even the governor himself pointed out that Texas had seen more lynchings in 1920 than any other state in the union—or any other civilized country, for that matter. "Human life," he declared, "is the cheapest commodity in this state."

And a certain level of that lawlessness spilled onto the football field. A recent game between Bryan High School and Austin saw a mob of University of Texas students refuse to pay admission to the high school playoff semifinal game. They took what they wanted, rules be damned, and rushed the stands. They took possession of the bleachers like oil barons grabbing land from the locals. And as the game progressed, so did their borders. Hundreds of fans intermittently swarmed the field with little or no security to keep them off the grass.

Bryan's coach had assured East Tech and the media that should the Clevelanders come to Texas, the game would not be played in such a lawless manner. They were a rule-abiding club. And unlike others in the state, they never fielded ringers.

But for Jack, a trip to Texas would mean standing on the sideline at best. There would be no banquets and no dances. No celebrations by the local Black community. No small boy tossing a piece of candy to his idol. No tear of joy running down his cheek. This was Texas, which for all intents and purposes was an extension of the Deep South.

When the telegram arrived, Coach Willaman gathered the team. He explained the situation to them. A vote was called. They recalled how just a year earlier they had narrowly lost the national championship. Now Everett was out of the picture and East Tech was a stronger team. To play down in Texas would be a big deal, and their chances at walking away with the trophy were pretty good. It was most of the team's senior year. Champ, Swede, Norty, Johnny, and everyone but Jack would be allowed to play. But on the other hand, Jack "could not go to Bryan without being embarrassed." They were a team. They were the East Tech football team. They were a family, and they looked out for each other. The team voted unanimously to reject Bryan's offer. A trip to Texas, the national spotlight, a shot at a championship—they turned it all down. For Jack. One of his teammates summed it up to the local paper by saying, "He gave us the best he had—we owe it to him."

The news of the rejection reached across to Texas, and it was not taken kindly. A column titled "Ni\*\*er in Woodpile Prevents Big Clash" asked its readers, "Why not let John Trice, the Negro East Tech star play against Waco or Bryant? He would hardly last a trice anyway." The author, H. H. "Jinx" Tucker, who would become a well-known but controversial Waco sportswriter, answered his own question. He went on to suggest, "John Trice might be embarrassed in Texas before the game, but he would not be embarrassed after being carried off the field at Cotton Palace park." There was something else more definitive that would take place: "More than likely he would be embalmed."

Words like these may have been meant to be trifling, but in Texas, where lynch mobs burned young Black men alive, it could hardly be considered a joke. Jack and his team stood strong together in the face of racism. They turned down a second chance at the national spotlight and a national championship. Instead they all finished their senior year. There was East Tech movie night at B.F. Keith's theater. There was the football banquet at Cleveland's fancy Statler Hotel. College offers for the White players came in, the world opening up before them.

Jack, however, did not have the same opportunities. College football offers for boys like him were harder to come by. He said goodbye to his teammates—to Swede, Champ, and Norty, and to his best friend, Johnny. Jack was unsure when he would see Johnny again. Both the Behm brothers had received offers to play for Knute Rockne at the fabled Notre Dame and were eager to get started. Jack said goodbye to dour-faced Coach Willaman, who was looking to leave coaching and had a business job lined up in Columbus. It looked like their run together was over. Jack thanked Uncle Lee and Aunt Pearl as he boarded the bus back home to Ravenna and to his mother. The familiar spires of the wool factories greeted him upon his return. But there was also someone else waiting for him: Cora.

# 7

# Freshman Year
# and the Peanut Man

JACK GRADUATED FROM HIGH SCHOOL IN EARLY 1922 AND SET ABOUT preparing for college. At that time, students could graduate either early in the winter or later in the spring. Having studied agricultural science at East Tech and knowing his father's roots in Tennessee, Jack intended to help Southern Black farmers. In the nearly 50 years after Reconstruction, Black-owned farming grew rapidly. By 1920 there were nearly one million Black farmers in the United States. Jack wanted to give back. He wanted to be like George Washington Carver, whom he had heard a lot about. It was said this great man of color, a professor and inventor, had received a standing ovation in Congress.

George Washington Carver was born into slavery on a 240-acre farm in Missouri. Moses Carver, the landowner, had purchased George's mother, Mary, and father, Giles, in 1855. Nine years later, Mary gave birth to George, but unfortunately Giles did not live to see the birth of his son. When George was an infant, slave raiders came to the farm and kidnapped Mary, George, and his sister and sold them to a farmer in Kentucky. Moses Carver feared for their lives. He hired a neighbor to track them down, but they only succeeded in finding George. His mother's and sister's whereabouts were unknown. It was said they were dead, but rumors suggested they were still alive somewhere else. Moses was able to return the small child back to his home in Missouri in exchange for a racing horse valued at $300.

The Carvers took six-week-old George into their family and raised the baby as their own son. George was considered too weak to work the fields, so he spent much of his time with Moses's wife, Susan, who taught him sewing, cooking, and gardening. She also taught him about herbal medicine. As George grew into manhood, he continued to learn about plants and gardening. He made his way to Iowa, where he found an opportunity to enroll at Iowa State College as a botany student.

In 1894 Carver graduated, and it is believed he was the first African American to earn a bachelor of science degree in the United States. Impressed by his research on the fungal infections of soybean plants, his professors asked him to stay. He worked at the Iowa State Experimental Station identifying and treating plant diseases. In 1896 Carver earned his master of agriculture degree. From there he moved to the Tuskegee Institute in Alabama at the invitation of Booker T. Washington.

As Carver rode the train to Alabama, he was struck by what he saw out the window. In a 1941 radio broadcast, he recalled: "My train left the golden wheat fields and the tall green corn of Iowa for the acres of cotton." But what he saw was not the promised land of Black pioneering. He recalled, "The scraggly cotton grew close up to the cabin doors; a few lonesome collards, the only sign of vegetables; stunted cattle, boney mules; fields and hillsides cracked and scarred with gullies and deep ruts." As an agricultural scientist, he immediately recognized a lack of scientific understanding. To him, "Everything looked hungry: the land, the cotton, the cattle, and the people."

Carver understood that cotton was king, but it did nothing to replenish its lands. When cotton grew, it laid down shallow roots that did little to hold the soil together. As a result, cotton fields could erode quicker than if the land had been left alone. He soon realized that the cotton was not only harming the land but also the Black farmers who raised it. Sharecropping was still the business model of Southern landowners, where Black farmers would "rent" land in exchange for a cut of the crop. The agreements were precarious. If a farmer suffered a bad year, or was arrested for a minor crime, the landowner could put their plot up for sale. In fact, they could sell the land out from under their feet at any time. The Black farmers saw little incentive to invest in science or improve the soil.

Carver encouraged Black farmers to live off the land rather than spend their money on supplies such as paint or fertilizer. Those things could be made with what grew under their feet. They didn't need to move to New York or Chicago to earn money. They could do it by growing crops besides cotton. Peanuts, as Carver pointed out, could help fertilize the soil, not to mention their nearly 300 other uses. There were also hundreds of uses for sweet potatoes and soybeans.

With Carver as his lighthouse, Jack began saving money for college. He worked as a mechanic during the day and a factory security guard at night. He planned to enroll at Cleveland's Case School of Applied Science. Most colleges and universities at the time were devoted to the concept of a liberal arts education. Case was one of only a handful of colleges focusing on a polytechnic education. It would later merge with the Western Reserve University to form Case Western Reserve University. And while football was still something Jack enjoyed, and Case did have a team, it no longer was his priority.

What free time Jack had, he spent with his mother, her relatives, and Cora. Cora continued working at the mills with Anna. As Jack and Cora grew closer, he bought her a necklace that became one of her most treasured possessions. Talk of marriage and moving to Cleveland became more frequent, albeit hushed. It seemed like their path together was laid out before them. Then, one summer day, a stranger arrived in Ravenna asking for directions to the Trice residence. He seemed to know Jack, but no one else knew him. The man found his way to 809 West Highland Avenue and knocked on the door. Jack opened the door and found Coach Willaman standing on his doorstep. He brought with him an exciting offer.

Willaman had recently been hired as the new head football coach for Iowa State College. He had been chosen by the school's athletic council composed of faculty, students, and alumni and offered a three year contract. Frank, his younger brother was hired as his assistant coach. Coach Willaman had already contacted Johnny, Norty, Champ, and Swede. The first three agreed to join the team, but they wanted Jack to join them, especially Johnny. The Behm brothers had already received room assignments at Notre Dame and had been getting ready to play for Knute Rockne when Willaman showed up at their family's Cleveland apartment. Sam convinced them to come with him to Iowa. Swede, on the other hand, turned down the coach's offer. Instead he had chosen Willaman's alma mater, Ohio State, to stay closer to his father. That left only Jack. Willaman took the journey down to Ravenna, eager to reunite his team for a new adventure.

At the time of Jack's recruitment, sports had begun to take on a renewed importance in colleges, especially in Iowa. Attitudes about collegiate athletics were evolving. Just a few years earlier, a professor at Iowa State "who took a keen interest in athletics" and declared it was an important part of education "would have been ostracized."

By this time, physical training had gained broad acceptance as being healthy for a young, developing body. Just as studying was healthy for the developing brain, so too was exercise. Athletics provided just such an outlet. College games were also becoming an important and entertaining diversion for the student body and a source of pride for the school alumni. Administrators began to see additional financial and social value in attracting strong student-athletes to their colleges and universities. When teams do well, they receive attention in the press. And according to a *Des Moines Register* sports editor at the time, "There is no denying that advertising pays."

Iowa State football had its origins under football pioneer Glenn "Pop" Warner in the 1890s, when the school's Cyclones nickname rose into existence. The budding program began to realize glory with its 1920 football team. But in just two years, students and alumni could see the promising glow of a championship football team fading away. Its rival, the University of Iowa, was pushing them out of the way and taking over the spotlight. The echoes of "Fight, Ames, Fight!" were fading into the background, and they needed to do something about it.

Several editorials published in the yearbook lamented the lack of athletic-minded administrators. The student body was told at various assemblies that they should be "satisfied with defeats" and "tolerate inferior athletics." Students would pick up the local sports paper and find familiar names who started their athletic careers at Iowa State now garnering headlines for their rivals at Iowa or Nebraska. An effort by alumni to support athletes with jobs on campus was lambasted as "professionalizing college athletics." President M.J. Riggs of the alumni association countered this line of thought by describing the state of football as dire. He argued that a better football program would increase enrollment and help raise money for building programs such as the Memorial Union. "We have our backs against the wall," he said at a large convocation. "And we've got to fight!"

Willaman was charged with turning the school's football program around, and he was bringing with him his nationally ranked East Tech boys. When he showed up in Jack's house, he laid out the benefits of Iowa State, including its growing school of agriculture. It wasn't lost on Jack that one of his idols, George Washington Carver, was the school's first Black student. On top of that, Carver had also valued athletics and had been the school's first athletic trainer. If Jack accepted Willaman's offer, he would follow in Carver's footsteps as Iowa State's first Black student-athlete.

Jack knew a great offer when he heard one, but he would have to leave his family and friends behind, including his mother and Cora. Once again, a promising opportunity lay before him, carrying with it the greater burden of being the sole representative for his race. Whether he liked it or not, it was a role he was used to playing. And it was what he had planned to do at Case, only better. He could both play football and study animal husbandry. But first he had to talk to his mom.

Jack approached his mother, and the two spoke about his future. Anna approved of his move to Iowa—after all, she often pressed for him to make something better of himself. Jack also spoke to Cora. Her family's close family friend William Pew had been the head of animal husbandry at Iowa State before returning home to run his family's farm. He had received a top-notch agricultural education in Iowa and was well respected in town.

Cora didn't want Jack to leave her, but she knew there was something great growing inside Jack. She loved Jack but didn't want to stand in the way of a once-in-a-lifetime opportunity. Cora proposed a stipulation: Jack would start school in the fall of 1922, work, and save money. Then, with a small nest egg and a place for them stay,

Cora would join him in Ames for the next academic year. She could study home economics. She would learn to cook and keep house. Jack agreed. But there was something else they needed to do before he left: They needed to solidify their relationship. They needed to get married.

In the early 1900s, nearby Michigan was a destination for young Ohioans looking for a quick marriage. The state had no residency law for a marriage certificate, and the minimum age of 18 was low compared to most other states. There was also no witness requirement. It could be a secret marriage if so desired. But most important for Jack and Cora's new timeline, there was no 60-day waiting period.

While some Michigan counties specialized in 30-second nuptials, Monroe advertised its ceremonies as less of an assembly line and more of a private ceremony. Monroe was only 170 miles from Ravenna. The young couple could easily take a train from Cleveland along the shore of Lake Erie to Toledo. From there they could hop on the summertime Beach Line trolley and get off just over the state border. If they left Toledo in the morning, they could be at the courthouse steps in Michigan by early afternoon.

Monroe was home to Reverend Reuben Crosby, known as the "marrying parson." He averaged nearly 300 marriages a year, with his wife often acting as the witness. Although three out of four marriages in Monroe County were of Ohio residents, and not Michigan ones, Crosby assured the local paper it was because there were so few Methodist Episcopal ministers in Ohio. They were simply parishioners flocking to his church for their faith. Of course, the church was also conveniently located two blocks from the courthouse and visible from the Toledo-Monroe trolley.

On July 27, 1922, Jack and Cora arrived in Monroe. They joined two other couples from Ohio on the courthouse steps waiting to be married. Finally it was their turn. They each signed the necessary paperwork, and by the powers of Reverend Reuben Crosby, they became husband and wife.

Two months later, Jack arrived in Ames. Buses were still few and far between, so Jack traveled to Iowa by train. After transferring in Chicago, he rode the Chicago & North Western Railroad line across the Midwest to downtown Ames. Skyscrapers quickly gave way to large swathes of farmland dotted with silos and smokestacks.

Ames was a town of 10,000 people, and nearly half the population was composed of the students and staff of Iowa State College. Most of the city's businesses and the train depot were located in downtown Ames, about two miles east of campus.

To help guide them in their new journey, Jack and the rest of the incoming class received a brown pocket-sized freshman handbook provided by the YMCA/YWCA. The book was intended to imbue the newcomers with the "Ames spirit." It was something to be valued and taken seriously. Iowa State wasn't the place for revolutionaries or rebels, or for those steeped in negativity. The handbook made it clear that "the crabber and the knocker do not belong in Ames."

President Raymond Pearson provided an opening greeting for the manual, boldly declaring that there were five simple keys to success: health, knowledge, good social qualities, right spiritual qualities, and earnest purpose. He assured the class of 1927, "In this country success cannot be denied to the young man or young woman who has these keys." Two pages later, Pearson's words of advice were followed by the school's battle cry: Fight, Ames, fight! Its origins lay in a marching song by Iowa State men who served in the 168th Infantry during World War I. Later a poem converted the subjects to gridiron warriors who, on fourth down, "answered when honor called; Blazing her name with splendid deeds." Their warrior cry became the title of the piece and the spirit of the football team.

Alongside Jack, a wave of students arrived to Ames in late September 1922. Excitement was mixed with a dash of uncertainty and a pinch of chaos for the new arrivals. Welcoming committees composed of sophomores, the Big Sisters club, the YMCA, and the YWCA dotted the landscape around the railways and bus station. The greeters could be easily spotted by the FRESHMAN RECEPTION badges prominently displayed on their lapels. Hordes of trunks arrived on the trains, all boldly labeled with homemade tags indicating their final destination. Even so, a few trunks every year still found themselves in the wrong city or delayed. Those students who managed to spot their luggage being loaded onto trucks at the depot made sure to remember the name of the drayman who loaded it. They might need to track him down if their luggage went missing.

Servicemen in short haircuts and well-pressed clothes arrived clutching the discharge papers that waived their school registration fees. Young girls arrived, some in modest attire from small towns, others in shorter skirts hailing from bigger cities. Several guarded their paperwork closely. School records were key to demonstrating the credits they had already completed. A lucky few hoped to avoid taking the entrance exams slated to start in just a few days. Jack did not have that luxury; he would need to take the entrance exams.

Opening weekend was also marked by several social events, including YMCA and YWCA receptions for the men and women as well as the annual pushball contest—a game played with 2 teams, a 140-yard field, and a towering 6-foot ball. The rooming bureau at the YMCA filled up and spilled over with students looking to get housing as close to campus as possible. Landlords in town agreed to provide each student who rented from them a bed, linens, curtains, a table, a dresser, and two chairs—but only one rocker per two people. Sufficient heat would be provided for studying until 10:30 PM. One toilet and washbasin would be provided for every 10 people. Quiet hours would be expected after 8:00 PM on weekdays and after 11:00 PM on weekends.

It was an Iowa State College rule that no one could register for classes without first securing a room. Yet housing at the time was scarce, especially for women. Large wooden colonial structures were built to temporarily house the recent influx of female students. Even some male students resorted to crashing on a cot in the hallway of a building or temporarily sleeping in the park before school started.

Largely driven by the on-campus housing crisis, a burgeoning community was growing south of campus. Originally referred to as the Fourth Ward for its voting annexation and then Dogtown for a period of time, a concerted local effort succeeded in naming the haphazard layout Campustown. It was here that the overflow of students and professors from campus could find housing. Newly built Tudor-style fraternity houses were popping up like prairie dogs. Drugstores, social halls, and cafés trickled in, catering to the area's new residents.

Johnny, Norty, and Champ succeeded in finding housing close to school in Campustown prior to the start of the semester. Those students who already had rooms taken care of could casually arrive closer to the first Monday of classes, but for Black students such as Jack, finding a place to stay was more challenging. It represented an entrance exam unto itself.

At the time, there were only about 20 Black students enrolled at Iowa State, which represented less than one-half of 1 percent of the student body. While there was no official rule barring Black students from living on campus, the segregation customs of the day prevented them from finding dorm housing. Discrimination came in many disguises. Former Iowa State College president Albert Storms, a Methodist minister, had assured W. E. B. Du Bois and the NAACP that Black students were welcome to attend the college, but in the same breath he admitted it would be difficult to find suitable housing. "It is not always easy for a Negro student to find rooming and boarding accommodations," he wrote. "Except where there are enough to room and board together, as is the case with Filipinos and with students of other nationalities."

Downtown Ames was an emerging business center. New yellow cabs and red-top cabs dotted Main Street. Above the storefronts that lined the streets, second floors provided rooms for small-business offices, lawyers, doctors, and dentists. Several shop owners also lived above their stores while others rented the apartment spaces out to desperate students. These small flats became a housing refuge for many people of color. For example, 226 Main Street housed Woolworth's on the first floor and several Black students on its second floor.

One local Black family, the Martins, tried to provide a refuge of their own. As former slaves from the South, they had migrated north to Iowa in 1913. They built a craftsman-style bungalow for themselves and their 12 children in downtown, just a few blocks from the train depot. As their own children grew up, their home also grew to house many of the college's Black students. The Martins provided not only shelter but also much-needed mentorship to the young Black men and women of Ames. They became integral pillars of the African American support system for the community. Archie Martin, the patriarch of the family, had met with Iowa State's then-president, Raymond Pearson, on more than one occasion. At each of their meetings, Martin insisted that Black students be admitted into campus dorms.

While Jack did not find a room with the Martins, he did negotiate a room downtown in the newly constructed Masonic building on Douglas Avenue. The three-story neoclassical brick building was home to the Ames chapter of the Freemasons. Athletes were not provided with scholarships and freshmen were not eligible for student loans, so it was up to Jack to earn money for tuition and rent. The school handbook also advised new students against working and maintaining a full class load. Nevertheless, Jack needed to earn money for school, Cora, and his mother, so he secured two janitorial jobs—one in a downtown office building and one for the school's athletic department.

Although Ames was founded by abolitionist-minded New England settlers, the people of Ames had very little experience interacting with people of color. When George Washington Carver arrived 28 years before Jack, he was the only African American in town. Despite his academic prominence, Carver was not allowed to eat at the same table as his fellow White students. By the time Jack arrived, the background stench of racism and harassment had already permeated the nooks and crannies of the college town.

An electric streetcar connected the real world of downtown to the idyllic world of the college campus. Yet neither was free of society's blight. Prejudice even gave rise to incidents on the streetcar itself. Young Black boys would be hoisted out of their seats forcefully if seated near White women. Black women would be the subjects of insults and slurs while riding to their destination; they did not respond, for they did not think the law was on their side.

Moses Lawrie, a local African American cleaner, tailor, and activist, wrote a letter to the *Ames Tribune* editor wondering out loud if there was a different set of laws for Black and White folks in town. In his letter, he described daily life in Ames as a person of color: "Many things have happened in the last few months that, I am sorry to say, have caused me to loose [sic] some of my civic pride. ... The fair-minded white citizens of Ames would be astonished if they knew of the many slurs and insults heaped upon the Negro citizens almost daily. They are insulted in places of business, in street cars and on the streets."

On campus, at least one of the Black maids who cleaned the fraternity houses was repeatedly harassed by a White man standing in the bushes outside the house demanding a date every time she showed up to work. Like many African Americans, she hesitated to bring the matter to the police for fear of backlash. Nevertheless, she was encouraged and supported by several local Black Ames activists. Eventually she agreed and reported the man's behavior. He was caught in the act by the police, and the man's conviction and fine made the front page of the local newspaper.

Restaurants were also potential powder kegs of bigotry. Contrary to the state law forbidding denial of service to patrons based on their skin color, some restaurants outright refused to serve Black people. Across Iowa, towns were just as likely to ban jazz dancing as they were Black diners. For White students, eating arrangements were readily available in clubs, private homes, and public eating houses. There were also local restaurants and the cafeteria at the YMCA. Unfortunately, cultural attitudes didn't always align with legislative actions, and sometimes bigotry simply defied the law.

Walter Madison was just the third Black student to graduate from Iowa State, in 1914. He had earned an engineering degree and was integral to designing the city's plumbing system. His first plumbing and heating business was housed in the same Masonic building where Jack resided. Madison successfully filed several patents, including one for a "flying machine." His business was advertised on the front page of the local city directory. For all intents and purposes, he was a model citizen. In 1922, the same year Jack arrived in Ames, Madison took a client to a local restaurant on Main Street for lunch. The two men were seated at a table. They conversed and looked at their menus. Suddenly the owner of the establishment emerged and stood alongside the waitress next to their table. In no uncertain terms they informed the two businessmen that the establishment did not serve Black people.

Madison protested, but embarrassment soon took over. Despite all he had done for Ames, Madison was still the subject of racial discrimination. He left the restaurant, but not without seeking justice. Following the incident, he successfully brought a lawsuit against the restaurant owner.

Walking onto the 125-acre campus for the first time, Jack encountered many signs, but perhaps none was more prominent or ubiquitous than KEEP OFF THE GRASS. The sanctity of the sidewalks was paramount at Iowa State. The student handbook dedicated an entire section to sticking to the walkways. It warned against cutting across the lawns. Should a person dare to alter the "tradition of keeping to the walks" and disrespect the natural beauty of the school's flora, he would be in direct conflict with the pride of his peers. Students caught in the act of wandering off the paved path would face a "solid fence of disapproval." Punishment was often immediately manifested in the form of "stretching." Stretching had been officially adopted by the student body following a vote that outlawing hazing in 1913. An apparently acceptable alternative, stretching was seen as a "harmless" corrective action to rectify "recalcitrant freshmen." It was a means to lead them "back to the straight and narrow path"—both literally and figuratively, it seemed. Stretching involved four men each grabbing a limb of the wayward soul and hoisting him high in the air before shaking him "much in the manner that two men use in shaking out a blanket."

Several other freshman rules were also dictated in no uncertain terms to Jack and his Cleveland teammates. Freshman men were required to wear their maroon class caps from 8:00 AM to 6:00 PM every day but Sunday from the first day of school until after commencement. The freshman women received an *F* pin, which they wore on their sweaters every day until Thanksgiving. Despite their pride as former East Tech Carpenters, it was forbidden for Jack and his friends to wear their high school insignias. As for college emblems, such as the brass *A* for *Ames*, freshmen would not be permitted to wear them except solely on their honor sweaters.

All men were expected to dress the same way: woolen olive-drab military-style shirts and corduroy trousers comprised the official uniform of the school, with the goal of leveling men of various economic backgrounds. All were seen as indistinguishable and equal in the eyes of the student handbook. (Not mentioned was that one could not hide the color of one's skin, which stuck out from under the uniform.)

That fall, Jack and his fellow East Tech graduates arrived eager to play under their mentor and the man responsible for shepherding them to Iowa, Coach Willaman. However, under the rules of the Missouri Conference, freshmen were not permitted to compete in intercollegiate athletics. As a result, Jack, Johnny, Norty, and Champ could only play their first year on the freshman team. Varsity would have to wait.

All athletic teams at Iowa State College fell under the purview of athletic director Charles Mayser. Mayser was the former head football and wrestling coach at Iowa State. In fact, he was the man responsible for bringing wrestling to the school and its initial success. Uncle Charley, as he was called, was a mixed bag of sternness and playfulness. He seemed just at home driving young men to bring home wrestling championships as he did giving magic shows to children in the hospital. He was also in charge of strength and conditioning for the athletes of Iowa State. It was his goal to create a pipeline for varsity sports, and to do that he needed to generate interest in athletics. "Varsity teams cannot be expected to be strong if the new men coming into college each year do not begin at once to interest themselves in athletics," he wrote. Everyone was expected to come out and play. "Don't be bashful," he remarked. "You shouldn't be embarrassed to play. In fact, the opposite is true. You should be embarrassed if you don't come out for athletics."

Jack, Johnny, Norty, and Champ came out for freshman football in the fall of 1922. The freshmen's main role was as a scrimmage team for the varsity team. Each week the underclassmen were taught the plays of that week's upcoming varsity opponent. In turn, they would scrimmage the varsity as surrogates for the upcoming Saturday game. That all changed on October 25, when the freshman squad, for one night only, was allowed to play a full game against the varsity team. No predetermined plays. No standing by while the older players focused on their game. In the game, both Behm brothers scored touchdowns and Jack ran the very level of interference Willaman had been preaching to his varsity team all season. They seemed unstoppable, especially for freshmen. Harry Schmidt, rising junior and the future team captain, recalled Jack blocking him harder than he had ever been blocked before.

During the home games, Jack and his freshman teammates would gather on the sideline to cheer on the upperclassmen. There were firm rules to be adhered to during athletic contests at Iowa State. Student spectators were expected to wait until the other team finished their cheer before responding. Everyone was to stand when the varsity team entered the field. When the varsity team won a home victory, the freshman players on the sideline would rush across the campus in pursuit of the Victory Bell. The bell, originally used to rouse students at 5:30 AM and mark the time throughout the day, had taken on a new significance. Following the mad dash, whichever student reached the Victory Bell first would ring it announcing to Iowa, and the world, that the home team had won. When the varsity team wasn't playing, the freshmen were expected at the school pep rallies without exception. There they would hype the team up with cheers and chants before the rally culminated with the lighting of a large, crackling bonfire.

Despite playing a starring role in freshman football and track-and-field, Jack spent most of his time being seen but not heard. In society, those with more power tend to take up more space. They tend to be louder and be heard more often. Those with less power take up less space and are quieter. As a result, Jack, by the standards of the White people around him, was considered a "gentleman" who "spoke only when spoken to." Harry Schmidt would later recall, "[Jack] was a very good fellow. He didn't speak out much. He kept his place. He acted like any respectable Black man should in those days."

When he was working at the Ames gym, Jack would wait quietly outside the offices until invited in, and then his frame would fill the doorway. He would clean everyone's muddy shoes without a word. He gladly helped people remove their heavy winter coats when they entered the gym and helped them put them on when they left.

According to author Steven Jones, founder and director of the Jack Trice Legacy Alliance, one day during an employee meeting at the gym, Jack rose from his chair and quietly walked around the table taking each person's pencil. The other employees looked around at each other, a confused look taking over their faces. Trice slowly strode over to the pencil sharpener and sharpened each pencil. The other employees followed him with their eyes as he returned. He repeated his circle around the table, placing each pencil next to its previous owner, and sat back down in his chair without a word.

Jones also wrote about a time when Jack passed by his teammate Bob Fisher, who was with his mother. Jack did not say a word. He didn't even make eye contact, keeping his eyes fixed ahead. Fisher was confused as to why the normally cheerful Trice had ignored them. Fisher told Jones he "couldn't imagine why Jack wouldn't say something." But then it quickly dawned on him: Because Fisher was with his mother, Jack wasn't taking any chances of inappropriate social contact as a Black man. Fisher immediately called out to Jack, who stopped, turned, and beamed his bright smile back at them. He then joined Fisher and his mother in conversation.

Merl Ross, who was in charge of ticket sales at Iowa State, saw Jack as a shy young man. Nevertheless, he put Jack in charge of collecting money from students who bought football tickets with fake checks. They were called the Bleacher Gang. Looking to avoid confrontation, Jack let another student—the school's baseball catcher, Allen Boller— collect the debts.

Mayser had taken a liking to Jack and quietly given him his own key to the gym, so Jack would often work at his job until late in the evening. His friends occasionally asked him out to dinner, but he often politely declined. He didn't want to risk any trouble if they were seen eating with a Black person. Instead, Jack typically ate by himself late at night. The dinner special at the local café cost 25 cents, an hour's wage at the gym.

As winter arrived, the maple trees on campus lost their leaves. A fresh coat of snow nestled onto the rows of sycamores like a soft blanket. A lone large Christmas tree festooned with lights stood on the lawn across from the Central Building, which housed the president's office. The building's looming neoclassical columns flanked the massive steps to its entrance. The students gathered by the Christmas tree for the annual tradition of singing carols.

The temperature continued to drop on campus, and Lake Laverne froze over. So too did the relationship between the Central Building and the athletic department. A cold war had begun to form whose potential collateral damage included Willaman and the East Tech boys. In the months ahead, when the battle heated up, Willaman would find himself under fire.

As the college's athletic director, Charles Mayser was the leader for the department and, by hierarchy, Coach Willaman's boss. It was Mayser who wielded a heavy hand in budgets and the hiring and firing of football coaches such as Willaman. As universities across America began to realize that college football could provide much-needed revenue and publicity for a school, finding successful coaches grew in priority.

The symbiotic relationship between an athletic director and his head football coach was often mutually important for either's career longevity. Any changes in athletic leadership might jeopardize the coach's ability to build a football program. The program would need money from the alumni and the support of the administration to attract and develop top talent. Mayser felt he was lacking that support. He believed that the school's Athletics Council, the administrators who oversaw his department, were out of touch with the needs of a growing athletic program. In his opinion, he said, members of the council didn't know the difference between football and the Statue of Liberty. From what he witnessed, the only time they set foot in the gym was during convocation.

According to Mayser, he had worked hard to increase football coaching salaries and bring local high school tournaments to campus for public relations and to build a pipeline to bring high-quality coaches and players to Iowa State College. Yet he was often met with resistance from the administration, some of whom passed members of the athletic department on the street without even recognizing them. In addition, he saw athletes turning down offers to play at Iowa State simply because of its strict rules. One told him he was afraid if he attended the school, he would be kicked out for wearing a red tie. Another remarked he would be in trouble if he parted his hair wrong. Siblings of students were encouraged not to attend their brother or sister's alma mater. Even former successful athletes who went on to coaching would not send their own student-athletes to Iowa State. Mayser thought maybe the school needed to loosen up a little and listen to him more.

For years, President Pearson had been battling the growing idea that the rules at Iowa State were too rigid. Battle lines were being drawn between the students' sense of empowerment and entitlement and the administration's sense of righteousness and paternalism. These lines would last for decades to come. One of the earliest conflicts in the drawn-out war centered on a student request to increase the hours allowed for dancing. It was, after all, the 1920s and the age of jazz.

By the early 1920s, radio was everywhere, advances in women's rights were being discussed in the open, and prohibition was being enforced. The dress codes were being adjusted, and young women were wearing clothes they would have been sent home for just a few years earlier. Some of the rules dictating male and female visitors were being lifted as well to allow for more intersex interaction.

The jazz age was in full swing, and with it came new dance moves that would previously have led to student banishment. In 1882, for example, dancing was outright banned at Iowa State. But by the 1920s, Saturday night dancing was an integral part of campus social life and courtship. When the students approached the administration asking for later dancing hours, their request was denied. This did not sit well with the students, who organized a campaign against the overbearing administration. In one instance of rebellion, they turned off all the lights at one of the school dances. When the lights came back on, anti-administration pamphlets had been spread out across the recreational space. This act of defiance did not sit well with Pearson, who, in a letter to the student body, used it as an opportunity to discuss rules on college campuses in general. He pointed out that the postwar world was seeing an increase in lawlessness, and he hoped the students of Iowa State would not be following in those same footsteps. He resented the distribution of pamphlets calling the faculty and administration hurtful names and hoped a state school would find itself with more respect among its students. Even the pamphlets themselves lacked proper English, for goodness' sake.

Pearson understood that while Ames did not offer the big-city excitement of a place such as Chicago or New York, it did offer its students green spaces, a top-notch gymnasium, and large athletic fields. It was these things they should be focusing on—not dancing into the early hours of the morning. If the students could provide a list of wholesome entertainment choices, he would be happy to discuss them further. And, he pointed out, one should not overlook the fine Sunday services found in Ames. "Broad-minded and experienced men and women can differ in judgment on a proposition and yet be friends," he added.

But by early spring, the snow had melted and the flowers on campus began to bloom. And amid all this new life, the tense situation with Mayser and the administration emerged from its hibernation, loud and hungry. The front page of the *Ames Daily Tribune* roared in all-caps: ISC IN ROW OVER MAYSER.

Mayser's conflict with the administration had resulted in an "unofficial" request for his resignation by the school's Athletics Council. The group had met without student representatives present and while Mayser was on a trip to New York. Mayser's intentions on this particular out-of-town trip appeared up for speculation. Some people wondered if he was lining up a new job back East.

It was when Mayser returned to Ames that President Pearson presented him with an ultimatum. The two men met in Pearson's office. After considerable conversation, Pearson admitted that the council felt Mayser lacked a certain amount of "administrative ability." No specific examples were provided, which only further enraged Mayser. How could he disprove something without concrete examples to discuss! Pearson offered him several months of paid vacation if he left quietly. A lively discussion of contracts, legalese, and just cause capped off their unfriendly encounter.

Storming out of the Central Building, Uncle Charley refused to resign. He demanded to meet with the Athletics Council. The group acquiesced. They sat down with him but only to let him know their minds were already made up. It appeared they were not going to have a two-way conversation. Mayser grew frustrated. As far as he knew, he was doing a good job, and without well-defined issues to defend, it became a game of opinions. The group of administrators circled their wagons like soldiers under fire. Nothing he could do would change the situation.

As word spread across campus and into town of Mayser's imminent departure, a committee formed by notable alumni met and came out in support of him. The rising value of football had already begun to provide the athletic department with valuable political connections and much-needed financial support. The town mayor, for example, was a former Ames football star and, because of that, carried significant weight with the townspeople.

The athletes themselves wanted to keep their former coach in his job as athletic director. All the varsity lettermen on campus—including the captain of the football team, Ira Young—voted for a resolution asking Mayser to stay at the college, and an official commendation. The Double A's, as the group was called, placed all the blame for the situation at the feet of the school's administration and its Athletics Council.

It appeared, however, that no matter what support emerged for Mayser, the council refused to work with him any further. Either they needed to go or he did, and they were the ones in power. The administration controlled what happened with the school's athletic programs, not the students and a disgruntled faculty member.

President Pearson encouraged Mayser to move on for the good of the college. Coach Willaman, Jack, and the rest of the team waited to see what Mayser's—and possibly their own intertwined fates—would become. It was a decision that could affect them all. In a college athletic department, no man is an island unto himself. Just like a new president means a new cabinet in Washington, a new college athletic directors can often mean a new coaching staff is not far behind. Both Behm brothers had turned down an opportunity to play at the exalted Notre Dame in order to play under Willaman. Jack had left his mother and young wife in Ravenna with the hopes they could join him the following year under the impression he would play football for many years in Ames. Willaman himself had left the bustle of Cleveland for the fields of Iowa. If Mayser left, would Willaman, and by proxy the East Tech grads, continue to stay in Iowa? Disruptions in athletic department leadership have their ways of trickling down.

The issue remained at the top of the school's mind through the end of May 1923. An estimated 1,500 students and supporters marched on the houses of both the mayor and President Pearson in support of Mayser. In a new pattern that would become a model for generations at Iowa State, Pearson decided the issue was hot enough that it should be decided formally by the students themselves. A representative student group would hear cases from both Pearson and Mayser and decide on a recommendation. They would act as a legislative body of sorts—a student government with real power. Like any congressional hearing, evidence could be introduced and witnesses called.

Hoping to stay out of the political spotlight, Willaman was instead dragged into its center. What made matters worse was that Willaman didn't really like Mayser and, it turned out, was considering leaving. It was well-known that Willaman was brought to Iowa State not only for his coaching skill but because he would bring several star high school football players with him. That had certainly sweetened the deal. But it wasn't enough to get Mayser on his side.

Before his time at Iowa State, Mayser had been the head football coach at Franklin & Marshall College in Pennsylvania. When he came to Iowa State in 1915, he became its head football coach as well. But the alumni began calling for a coach who knew "twentieth-century football," and Mayser didn't fit that bill. And what the alumni and their money wanted, they usually got. Reluctantly Mayser stepped aside from coaching after only four years to become the athletic director.

And he didn't make it easy for his replacements. He reportedly forced out the two subsequent head football coaches after only one season each. One of Mayser's biggest critics was former football coach and college physician Norman Paine, who was the first coach Mayser had forced out. The friction of their relationship grew out of the death of Iowa State wrestler George Schilling. Schilling had died of a skin infection that spread through the rest of his body. It was Paine's opinion that Schilling contracted the disease due to Mayser's carelessness and disregard for the health of his athletes and the lack of cleanliness at the gym. Furthermore, Paine had written in his resignation letter to Pearson that Mayser offered no cooperation with the football staff. It seemed he preferred to let that die too. Mayser, of course, denied these accusations and felt he was a scapegoat of poor doctoring and a lack of support by the Athletics Council.

Unsurprisingly, given Mayser's track record with the coaches who followed him, a rumor had begun circulating around campus that Sam Willaman was considering leaving after his first season as well. Apparently to some, "Sad" Sam was no Knute Rockne. Willaman didn't want news of his impending departure getting out, especially to Jack, Champ, and the Behms. It would devastate them if they knew he was leaving.

Early on, Willaman felt his own relationship with Mayser had become strained. Part of it involved hiring his brother Frank. He had brought Frank with him after the younger brother finished up his playing career at Ohio State. Mayser thought Frank should be let go and a new line coach hired at a cheaper salary, which didn't sit well with Coach Willaman.

Another area of concern for Willaman was that he hadn't immediately turned the varsity team around, something expected of coaches throughout history. Despite Willaman's three-year contract, he began to worry that he had failed in his first season as varsity coach. Even with Jack, Champ, and the Behm brothers joining the varsity team the next season, Willaman was worried he would fail again if he didn't better understand how to navigate the choppy waters in which he and Mayser found themselves.

Unsure what to do with the situation, Willaman wrote a letter to Norman Paine asking for advice. Willaman admitted to the former coach he could leave if he needed to. He could get another job with a better salary, even, but his performance at Iowa State was a matter of pride, for both him and his protégés. He had always found himself surrounded by successful teams and organizations and could not derive self-satisfaction if he wasn't getting the maximum possible results. He wondered if Paine could provide any advice.

In closing, he said he trusted Paine would keep his letter confidential. Unbeknownst to Willaman, Paine had forwarded the letter to one of the school deans, citing it as an example of yet another football coach— even one who he termed a complete stranger to himself—"struggling against the kaiser's iron heel." Paine penned a reply to Willaman relaying his own history with Mayser and cautioned him that, while educators preferred "clean" sports in the 1920s, townspeople and alumni just wanted winning teams. The mission statement, it appeared, was to win at all costs.

This letter Willaman wrote to Paine was a key piece of evidence introduced in Mayser's hearing before the student representatives. After more than five hours of hearings, the student committee ultimately agreed it was in the best interest of moving everyone involved if Mayser agreed to resign. But in exchange for his resignation and the students dropping their protests, an entirely new Athletics Council would be established. Unlike before, when student interests were ignored, the new council would need to include a sizable representation of students, both athletes and nonathletes. The students at Iowa State wanted a voice when it came to athletics—a voice that would not be silenced. It would not be the last time the students demanded to be heard when it came to decisions on athletic issues, and certainly not the biggest.

With his appeal officially denied, Mayser reluctantly agreed to step down as Iowa State athletic director. He arranged to reclaim his former position at Franklin & Marshall College. All was not lost for Mayser, however, for he went on to establish a coaching career that led to the National Wrestling Hall of Fame.

Willaman, on the other hand, was still hoping to turn the team around. He decided to stay on as head coach and kept his brother Frank with him on staff. Having navigated the muddy waters of athletic department politics, Willaman was ready to see Jack, Johnny, and Norty become the team's future stars and the Cyclones become the state's best football team. With the end of the school year on the horizon, the former East Tech Carpenters would finally be eligible for Cyclones varsity football.

Willaman also hired several new coaches, including a semi-professional player and line coach from the University of Minnesota and a new freshman football coach who would end up having a strong influence on Jack's life perspective. Off the field, the new freshman team coach would soon help Jack see there was something greater than himself—that he had a higher calling. But first Jack had to prove himself on the field.

May of 1923 saw Coach Willaman's first major football tryout. More than 160 men came out for six weeks of training. Each hopeful was ranked on several football skill tests, including running, passing, receiving, and blocking. Johnny and Norty tied at first place for the 100-yard dash while carrying a football. Jack came in fourth. Still, all three rising sophomores recorded impressive 100-yard-dash times, each one coming in around 11 seconds. (For reference, a decade later, while at East Tech, future Olympian Jesse Owens would set the high school 100-yard dash record in 1933 by tying the world record of 9.4 seconds.) In a testament to their overall speed, Johnny and Norty also tied for first in open-field running. Jack continued to lay claim to the title where his greatest physical talents lay: He was ranked first for blocking and interference. When the six weeks were up, Johnny, Norty, and Jack had earned their spots on the varsity team.

Notably absent from spring scrimmages was the fourth member of the East Tech squad, Champ Hardy. Toward the final weeks of winter, the former senior class president described by the yearbook staff as "a champ in name and a champ in deed, whatever the task he is sure to succeed" had begun feeling run-down. At first he felt like he just had the flu. Then he began to have ear trouble. After nearly two months of being sick off and on, during which time he also had a sinus operation, an empyema had formed inside Champ's chest, filling his lung cavity with pus. His oxygen levels began to drop and he struggled to breathe. Champ was admitted to the new on-campus hospital, but on March 22, 1923, his body finally lost its battle against the invading bacteria. Before even playing a single varsity game, Champ died. He became the first but not the last member of the East Tech boys to die at the campus hospital.

Funeral services were held at the local Duckworth's undertaker parlor. The tragedy devastated Willaman. His philosophy had always been, "The boy comes first, the school second, and the public third." Champ was a promising young athlete and only 20 years old. Now one of Willaman's boys was dead. Losing one of his players who was so young and promising, especially one whom he knew so well, must have pained him deeply. Jack, Johnny, and Norty also mourned their longtime friend. They had spent five years laughing with and playing alongside Champ. Suddenly he was gone from their lives. Their original group of four was now down to three.

Even in the wake of Champ's death and Mayser's resignation, May 1923 still brought a celebration of life and renewal for Jack and the rest of the team. The second annual VEISHEA arrived to distract them. It was a student-run celebration of spring that would go on to become one of the school's most prominent, and notorious, celebrations. The VEISHEA had received its name from an acronym of the five divisions of Iowa State: Veterinary Medicine, Engineering, Industrial Science, Home Economics, and Agriculture. The year before, the inaugural celebration had included a parade, open houses for each school at the college, a horse show, and the naming of the VEISHEA queens. In

1923 the students added additional evenings of shows, music, and dancing.

Jack's first VEISHEA lasted three days. Classes ended at noon on the first day so the festivities could kick off. The first of two Iowa State–Nebraska baseball games was played, followed by a dance and a performance of the comic opera *The Pirates of Penzance*. Cherry pies were given out, a tradition that would be repeated each year.

Visitors arrived by car and train. Many of them were parents of Iowa State students who came to see their children and tour the campus. There is no evidence Anna came to see Jack. The whole university was set up as an open house. In addition, nearly 650 high school athletes had come to Ames to compete in golf, tennis, and track tournaments. The town was packed to its brim with people.

On the morning of the VEISHEA parade, large crowds packed the sidewalks eager to see the colorful floats. It was the largest parade Ames had ever seen. It stretched for three-quarters of a mile and showcased 60 unique floats. The colorful caravan first wound itself around the Iowa State campus and then made its way down Lincoln Way toward downtown Main Street. Children, residents, and businessmen waved and cheered from the periphery.

Each division at Iowa State entered a float. The mechanical engineering float featured a live statuary. The home economics float was colorfully decorated to showcase the students' artistic skill set. The physical education department entered its own float showing off its namesake with several fit and energetic young women on board demonstrating the latest exercise techniques. The agricultural float, titled "The Magic of Milk" puttered along, seemingly weighed down by all the trophies the department had accumulated as one of the nation's best schools. Men in milkman outfits walked along its side.

Then came the fraternities, each one overflowing with people in a convertible car. Two bands marched along the route while a jazz band played to revelers dancing at the parade's finish line. It was a celebration encompassing a time when a pandemic and a World War had just passed. Alcohol may have been banned in Ames, but dancing and music were still legal.

The VEISHEA played a significant role on Iowa State's campus until 2014, when it was officially retired as an event in the wake of numerous problems over the preceding 26 years. Riots during VEISHEA in 1988, 1992, 1994, 2004, and 2014 (and a murder in 1997) sealed the event's fate, and as of this writing it is unlikely to return.

But for Jack and his now-varsity teammates and friends in 1923, it must have felt like a welcome reprieve after the tragedy of Champ's passing and the uncertainty they had endured during Mayser's ouster. Little did anyone know, it would be the only VEISHEA Jack would have the pleasure of attending.

# 8

# Alpha Phi Alpha and Varsity Football

THAT SUMMER, JACK RETURNED HOME TO RAVENNA PROUDLY WEARING a No. 26. When a freshman athlete excelled in a sport, he was given a numeral award signifying the year he would graduate. For Jack, it was 1926. The Behm brothers and the late Champ Hardy were also among the 20 recipients of football numerals. Jack also brought home to Ravenna the conference championship in shot put. But Jack wanted something else. He wanted a big *A*—the varsity letter. And for that he would need to play at least three varsity football games.

He spent a few weeks at home with his mother before returning to Ames. By the beginning of August, Jack had already arrived back at school to begin training for the upcoming varsity football season (The *Cedar Rapids Gazette* has Jack there by the beginning of August.) That summer, as promised, Cora also moved in with him in the downtown apartment in the Masonic building. She registered for home economics classes in the fall. So she could learn to feed the ever-growing Jack better, she joked.

It was a hot summer, and with the Midwest temperatures rising, Jack looked for a way to cool off between work and football. There was the spray pond at the municipal electric plant, but that was mostly for children. The town swimming hole, Carr Pool, wouldn't open until 1926. And even then, Black people would only be allowed to swim in the chilly early mornings before the pool officially opened to White people. Instead Jack took advantage of his key to the State Gymnasium and its own swimming pool. The year before, he had learned to swim through the school's recently formed American Red Cross Volunteer Life Saving Corps. He could use the school's pool to practice and get fit. On rare occasions, Cora would also join him for a late-night romantic dip.

Summers in Ames featured multiple concerts and lectures on campus for the students and townspeople to attend. Topics at that time ranged from astronomy to Prohibition. The summer of 1923 also saw back-to-back lectures on propaganda and its effectiveness as a new and powerful tool for social progress. The modern fight for personal righteousness was also a major topic of discussion.

The July 4, 1923, program featured the Cotton Blossom Singers of the Piney Woods School. The group hailed all the way from Piney Woods, Mississippi, 23 miles southeast of Jackson. Their performance was billed as "a Concert of Negro Melodies."

Piney Woods was the home of several talented gospel groups that would later influence the sounds of both James Brown and Ray Charles. The Cotton Blossom Singers were the brainchild of Laurence Clifton Jones, who sent the group out on an annual fundraising tour across the nation, and they made frequent stops in Iowa. No admission was charged for the concert, but a collection was taken up at the door.

Laurence Jones had himself graduated from Iowa in 1907 before turning down a chance to teach at the famed Tuskegee Institute alongside George Washington Carver. Instead he chose to settle in the Piney Woods area of Mississippi. Like Jack after him and Carver before him, he had set his sights on using his agricultural education to help Black farmers in the South. He established a school for young Black children whom he saw as individual trees of a "human orchard," and he saw it as his job to nurture and "spray" them.

In the beginning, Jones had no missionary society support or other financial backing. Instead his school began with a donation by a former slave of 40 acres of land. From there, Jones worked hard to establish interest in his school and relationships between farmers and financiers in both Iowa and Mississippi. It was said that he was such a great orator that even Dale Carnegie included his story in at least one of his books. According to Carnegie, a mob had been sent to lynch Jones. But by the time Jones was done speaking, he had convinced the mob sent to hang him to donate to his school instead.

Jones's hard work resulted in nearly 170 acres of land available for the agricultural training of young Black men and women. One or two of Jack's own professors knew Jones personally and had helped establish the school in its early days. Jones was another person to look up to in Jack's pantheon, alongside George Washington Carver. Still, Jack wanted to do more than *read* about successful Black men; he wanted to *be among* them. To be friends with them. Fraternities, it seemed, could provide that opportunity.

The second half of freshman year was the time when fraternities began to extend membership offers, but it was in a student's sophomore year when he could become a full-fledged brother. As to the question of whether a Cyclone student should join a fraternity or social club, the 1923 student handbook offered this advice: "Your college companionships will have much to do with your success as a student and also the making of your character... Therefore choose the associates who have the principles and ideals which you want to dominate your life."

Jack's friends from Cleveland had found their own social circles among the White fraternities. Norty—and Champ before his death—had both pledged SAE. Johnny would become a member of Phi Kappa Psi. (He also had the honorable distinction of joining the Pebbles, a select group of inter-fraternity athletes of small stature.) These organizations, however, did not extend invitations to minorities such as African Americans and Jews. As a result, those minority groups sought to create their own Greek letter organizations. On Thanksgiving of Jack's freshman year, Alpha Phi Alpha became the first Black fraternity at Iowa State. When he returned as a sophomore, he was eager to join their second-ever class.

Alpha Phi Alpha had been established in 1906 on the campus of Cornell University in New York. In fewer than 20 years, it had branched across the country, embracing men of color into its fold. By 1923 there were 49 chapters and more than 3,000 members. The organization provided a support network that would continue to build some of the nation's most prominent Black leaders for more than 100 years. Its motto remains "First of All, Servants of All, We Shall Transcend All."

The Alpha Nu chapter at Iowa State boasted future Black leaders even among its earliest ranks. At least two of Jack's new fraternity brothers, Rufus Atwood and Jesse "J. R." Otis, would go on to become college presidents. Charles Preston Howard would graduate from Drake Law School and cofound the National Bar Association. Another brother, Lawrence A. "L. A." Potts, wrote and directed a play while in school titled *Robbers and Murderers* that highlighted the concept that mental robbery is more prevalent than physical. He then went on to become the director of the Division of Agriculture at Prairie View State College, the first state-supported African American college in Texas, and dean of the School of Agriculture at Tuskegee University from 1946 to 1962.

One of jack's elder fraternity brothers, Frederick Douglass Patterson, was the only Black Iowa State student enrolled in veterinary medicine at the time. He went on to found the United Negro College Fund and serve as president of the Tuskegee Institute for nearly 20 years. He also received the Presidential Medal of Freedom.

Black fraternities at Ames weren't offered the newly built Greek housing that other fraternities and sororities enjoyed, so like Jack, members lived downtown in various shared apartments. Otis, Atwood, Potts, and Patterson lived together in a small apartment at 202½ East Main Street above a downtown ten-cent store, packed together with several more Alphas and other Black students, according to Lea E. Williams' *Servants of the People.*

The roommates of this particular domicile hailed from several faraway states. Otis was from Mississippi, Atwood was from Kentucky, Potts was from Florida, and Patterson was from Texas. Their journeys had brought them together in the center of the country, and fittingly, the group nicknamed themselves the Interstate Club. Costing 16 dollars a month, the apartment included a small kitchen and dining room, a front room for socializing, and a larger room in the rear for sleeping. Many of the roommates were recently discharged from the army, so to fit all their beds in the small space, they lined them up in the familiar style of army barracks. Every cent counted, and as a result, most of the time the students living downtown walked the mile to campus rather than paying for the streetcar.

While the members of Alpha Phi Alpha enjoyed their time in Ames, there wasn't much room for a social life. Many of them worked long evening hours. Jobs were necessary but ever changing. As racial attitudes and preferences waxed and waned, so too did job descriptions.

Many of the Alphas rotated between serving food in hotel restaurants and sorority houses to performing cleaning and janitorial duties. At one point, Otis and Patterson set up and ran their own downtown laundry business, complete with a hobbling delivery truck. After work, many of the men studied deep into the night. Textbooks weren't readily available, so most of what they learned was from notes taken during lectures.

Jack's closest friend from the fraternity, Harold L. Tutt, would rise to become the chapter's vice president. He had been raised by his grandmother in Missouri, and he was a sports fan who loved coaching kids. The Alpha Nu chapter was small but proud; it promoted its members' accomplishments in whatever platform was provided. In just a few months of membership, Jack's name was mentioned several times in the national fraternity newsletter, the *Sphinx*.

As part of his community service mission, Jack started the Jack Trice Club, aimed at improving the moral and physical character of young boys in Ames. This was part of a national Alpha Phi Alpha campaign named Go-to-High-School, Go-to-College. The motto for the campaign was "The Future of Our Race Is Dependent Upon the Education of Our Boys and Girls." Brothers were charged with spreading their message to every high school and as many Black communities as possible either by personal contact or through distribution of educational materials. Jack's chapter focused on speaking after local ministers' sermons. They also held a dinner for local high school seniors, at which several of the brothers gave talks. In one year alone, it was estimated that the fraternity reached more than two million children across the U.S. with their message.

As an Alpha, Jack found a home among college-educated Black men who strove to lift up those around them. To be an Alpha man meant to live a life of honest devotion and brotherly love. His mother's desire for him to be around other people of color and his own age finally saw its greatest fulfillment not in Cleveland but in Ames. He could finally let the mask slip down. It was among his fraternity brothers that Jack could discuss the difficulties he and they faced. They discussed racial discrimination and progress in the United States. They questioned how they could help their less fortunate brethren in the South. They sought out humble faith and noble goals. They strove to be a credit to people of color. Far from the little Black boy in Hiram with crocodile tears, Jack had grown tremendously—not only physically but also spiritually.

Between classes, work, and the Alphas, Jack joined Johnny, Norty, and another Clevelander—"Spike" Nave, from Shaw High School—on the field. In the off-season, Willaman had acquired lighter, more efficient football pads and changed the team's jerseys to feature more gold. "We must have one ambition," he wrote to the football players in a letter. "To be the best team Ames ever had." Jack, meanwhile, had grown to more than 200 pounds and wielded the strength of a fully grown man.

ISC's football line coach was an imposing, square-jawed figure named George Hauser. He took a train each Sunday from Iowa to Chicago to play for a professional football team. That team became the NFL's Chicago Bears. Even as only a sophomore, Jack noticeably held his own one-on-one against the pro-footballer Hauser. As Johnny Behm remembered to the *Cleveland Plain Dealer* decades later, sometimes the bigger man would ask Jack to stay after practice. The two of them would train together, making each other better. Steel sharpening steel. If Jack could challenge a professional in just his second year of college, perhaps his own professional career in football wasn't much of a stretch. Each scrimmage, it would take two or three men to contain Jack. The school paper pronounced that opposing teams were going to have their hands full closing the holes Jack was sure to open.

Standing on the sideline, the new freshman football coach, William Thompson, watched Jack give "everything he had" on the field. But it was off the field and after practice where a strong connection grew between the two men. Thompson's worldview was shaped by being a Presbyterian minister who had graduated college with a degree in psychology. These two attributes lent themselves well to inspiring young athletes.

According to a letter written by Thompson in 1974, he would often spend time talking with Jack about football and life. Their discussions would be friendly but always serious and on a superior level. Jack impressed the young academic and philosopher with "the fact that he was dedicated and idealistic." He loved football "for what it taught him of manhood" but like many football players after him, Jack was determined to focus on the "worthy causes which would be open to him because of a good education."

The team's first game of the 1923 football season was scheduled against a smaller school, Simpson College. It was seen by most as a warm-up game. The opening half began with a literal bang: military cannons signaled the start of the season. On paper, Simpson didn't pose much of a challenge. Yet for Jack and many of the other boys, it was the first of the three varsity games they needed to letter.

At first Iowa State failed to live up to its expectations as a "flashy" team. The field was muddy and the ground slippery. Simpson managed to put early pressure on the Cyclones. They brought the ball within 12 yards of the end zone. It wasn't until Jack scrambled to the front of the line and blocked a dropkick that the Cyclones managed to turn the game around. Before the first half ended, Johnny managed to catch a pass and run 70 yards for the first touchdown of the game.

The second half continued to be a physical battle. Jack managed to force a fumble, recovering it for Iowa. In a hard-fought game, the Cyclones relied on the "Willaman aerial attack" and held the lead until the very end, winning 14–7. The *Iowa State Student* graded Jack as ranking "by far the most outstanding performer." Sweaty and tired, nearly 14 pounds lighter than when he started the game, Jack helped lead "a spirit of fight not shown on State field for some time." Simpson, on the other hand, crumbled under the physicality of Willaman's team. They left the field with five of their starters injured.

Following the Simpson victory, the Cyclones turned their sights north toward the University of Minnesota. The Gophers were developing into a powerhouse team, and the Ames-Minnesota contest was considered one of the most important games of the early football season. William Spaulding oversaw the Gophers football squad. Before their own season opener against Ames, Minnesota was still struggling to fill their starting lineup. Several of their starters were on the injured list, then referred to as the "hospital list." Two of their stars were also questionable due to academic concerns. Exams were scheduled days before the matchup that, if passed, would allow the additional men to take the field. A lot of pressure had begun to build, as the Minnesota team was expected to become a major player in the Big Ten.

Spaulding was a stern-faced man who had a long history of football excellence. Beginning in college, he helped lead his small college team to an unexpected win against the powerhouse Notre Dame in 1905. He then had a short stint as a professional football player before becoming the winningest coach in the history of the Western State Normal School (later renamed Western Michigan University). He coached the team there for 15 years before being hired to lead the University of Minnesota in 1922. His legacy would later include coaching UCLA football for more than 10 years, including a young Jackie Robinson, before becoming the school's athletic director.

As in years before, Jack, Johnny, Norty, and Coach Willaman left for the train station on the heels of thousands of fans and the sounds of the school band. This time, however, something felt different to Jack. Before they headed to the depot, Jack asked to stop back home. He wanted to see Cora before they left. He needed to tell her something.

Jack ran up the stairs of the Masonic building. He had to say goodbye to Cora. Jack breathlessly reached Cora and hugged her. He wrapped her up in his big frame. Their lips met in a kiss. It was an embrace she would remember for the rest of her life. "I will come back to you as soon as I can," he whispered. His coach called up after him. With those words hanging in the air, Jack left.

MARGARET SMITH,
5608 Kinsman Ave.

JOE WHITMAN,
15001 Ridpath Ave.
Spanish Club
Aggies

*She did in three years with honor*
*What it took us four to do.*

JOHN TRICE,
3324 E. 126th St.
Football
Track

*Brevity? You'll always be short,*
*eh, Joe?*

*His smile and his tackle*
*How they comfort us.*

CARL UNDERWEGER,
10309 Ostend Ave.
Freeman Wreckers
Student Council

*We don't know what your name*
*means, Carl,*
*But it sounds substantial, just*
*like you.*

ARTHUR J. WILTSHIRE,
9821 Heath Ave.
Commencement Speaker
Secretary Freeman Wreckers
Student Council

*In smiles and compliments*
*bedight*
*You make a perfect gentle*
*knight.*

DONALD VALENTINE,
12025 Woodland Ave.
Freeman Wreckers

*Silent come and silent go;*
*Here's a chap you'd like to know.*

*Jack's senior photo at East Tech High School*
*in Cleveland.* (CLEVELAND PUBLIC LIBRARY)

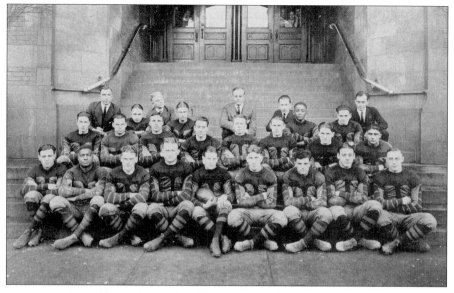

*Jack (front row, second from left) was a standout on the state champion football team.* (Cleveland Public Library)

OHIO STATE CHAMPIONS

*Jack (front row, second from left) was also a member of the state champion track team.* (Cleveland Public Library)

*Jack, Champ
Hardy, and the
Behm brothers at
East Tech in 1921.*

*And in 1923 at Iowa State.*

*Jack flashes his trademark smile.*

*The 1923 Iowa State Cyclones football team.*

Oct 5, 1923

To Whom it may concern:—

My thoughts just before the first real college game of my life. The honor of my race, family, & self are at stake. Everyone is expecting me to do big things. I _will_! My whole body & soul are to be thrown recklessly about on the field tomorrow. Every time the ball is snapped I will be trying to do more than my part. (supper)

On all defensive plays I must break thru the opponents line at stop the play in their tracks. Watch out of pass interference. Fight low with your eyes open and toward the play. Roll block the interference. Watch out for cross bucks and reverse end runs. Be on your toes every minute if you expect to make good. (meeting) at 7:45—

Jack

*Jack's last letter.*

*Thousands of people gathered on campus to
pay tribute to Jack at his funeral.*

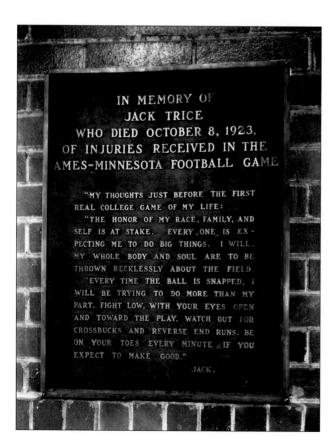

IN MEMORY OF
JACK TRICE
WHO DIED OCTOBER 8, 1923,
OF INJURIES RECEIVED IN THE
AMES-MINNESOTA FOOTBALL GAME

"MY THOUGHTS JUST BEFORE THE FIRST
REAL COLLEGE GAME OF MY LIFE:
"THE HONOR OF MY RACE, FAMILY, AND
SELF IS AT STAKE. EVERY ONE IS EX-
PECTING ME TO DO BIG THINGS. I WILL.
MY WHOLE BODY AND SOUL ARE TO BE
THROWN RECKLESSLY ABOUT THE FIELD.
EVERY TIME THE BALL IS SNAPPED, I
WILL BE TRYING TO DO MORE THAN MY
PART. FIGHT LOW, WITH YOUR EYES OPEN
AND TOWARD THE PLAY. WATCH OUT FOR
CROSSBUCKS AND REVERSE END RUNS. BE
ON YOUR TOES EVERY MINUTE IF YOU
EXPECT TO MAKE GOOD."

JACK.

*The plaque
that started a
movement.*

### The Jack Trice Controversy

"Basically, we're trying to combat ignorance about Jack Trice and his ideals," said Jeff Elliott, chairman of the Jack Trice Memorial Foundation.

In keeping with this, the Foundation carried the fight to have the football stadium, commonly referred to as "No Name Stadium" by Iowa State University students and faculty, named after Jack Trice. Trice was Iowa State's first black athlete and ISU's only athlete to die of injuries sustained during competition. In a continuing effort to gain support for having the stadium named after him, a tailgate was given before the ISU-Oklahoma football game on Nov. 19. Black arm bands and literature about Jack Trice were distributed. Also, ISU Band members were asked to wear white arm bands on their uniforms during the game.

The Jack Trice Memorial Foundation has been working to gain support for having the stadium named "Jack Trice Memorial Stadium." The State Board of Regents, however, supports naming the stadium simply "Cyclone Stadium." This proposal has drawn a lot of criticism from students, faculty and alumni.

Since 1974, there has been an intense drive to have the stadium named for Jack Trice.

The proposal has since been endorsed by the Government of the Student Body, the Interfraternity Council, the Student Union Board and the Councils of the Engineering and Home Economic colleges. Also, signatures have been obtained from 3,000 to 4,000 students, faculty and alumni supporting the Jack Trice proposal.

Despite this, however, the administration continued to support "Cyclone Stadium." President W. Robert Parks recommended the decision to the State Board of Regents.

The Board of Regents refused to take action on the naming of the stadium until March, after the stadium's been paid off.

**Michael Morris, photographs by Klaus Kocher**

*Editor's note* — The stadium was named "Cyclone Stadium" and "Jack Trice Field" during finals week of fall semester 1983.

*Above left: The first black athlete at ISU, was Jack Trice. The significance behind this name is the fact that he was the only school athlete to die of injuries sustained during competition. Middle: This is just one example of the Jack Trice publicity that was often seen prior to football games. There were many tailgates in the parking lots promoting the idea of "Jack Trice Memorial Stadium." Above: White and black arm bands were worn at the ISU-Oklahoma game to signify one's support of naming the stadium after Jack Trice. Many fans and students wore these, as did many ISU band members while performing at halftime.*

*Happenings / 131*

A September 29th Movement protest poster.

ISU's yearbook coverage of the Trice controversy in the 1983–84 *Bomb*.

Milton McGriff addresses the crowd during a September 29th Movement press conference in 1997. (Bob Modersohn/Des Moines Register-Imagn Content Services, LLC)

*This statue of Jack, dedicated in 1988, now stands outside the stadium named for him.*

*On any given Saturday, Jack Trice Stadium can hold more than 60,000 Cyclones fans.* (ISTOCK.COM/CRobertson)

# 9

## Jack's Letter

THE TEAM TOOK THE TRAIN NORTH TO MINNESOTA. JUST LIKE IN HIGH school, Jack and Johnny ate together and slept near each other. Their friendship continued to remain strong despite their broadening worlds. The train took them to Minneapolis. The team made its way to Northrup Field, where they ran through a practice that was closed to the public. From there, sweaty and tired, they traveled downtown to settle into their hotel rooms for the night.

When they arrived in downtown Minneapolis to check into the Curtis Hotel, there was already tension in the air—not just because of the football game but something else, something palatable. It was a bitterness many of the young White boys from farm country hadn't tasted before. They had heard about racism but never really witnessed it firsthand. Perhaps they had been blind to it or willfully ignorant. Now, in the middle of a big city, they could tell something was different.

Minneapolis had been struggling with a racial reckoning. It was a tug-of-war within the heart of the state. In 1920, just three years earlier, a White mob had lynched three Black men in nearby Duluth when they wrongfully believed the circus employees had raped a White girl. This recent rise in lynchings had motivated the state to pass the nation's first anti-lynching law in 1921. And yet it was only two years later that the Ku Klux Klan ran a strong campaign for the 1923 mayoral race of Minneapolis. At least 10 Klan groups were reported to be active in Minneapolis, and their first newspaper, *The Voice of the Knights of the Ku Klux Klan*, was published in early 1923. By the end of the year, Minnesota would be home to more than 50 chapters boasting 30,000 members. Even the University of Minnesota permitted a Klan float to join its 1923 homecoming parade. It depicted a large robed horse, a hooded man, and a shotgun.

Not all racism was advertised with hatred. Some of it was wrapped in the veil of business. It wasn't until 1924 that the Phyllis Wheatley House would be established in Minneapolis. The social services center housed Black students who were not permitted to live in the University of Minnesota dorms. It also provided lodging to Black luminaries who otherwise might not find lodging while visiting the city, including Langston Hughes and W.E.B. Du Bois.

In that vein, many Minneapolis hotels did not permit Black patrons to stay in their rooms; others allowed them to sleep in their beds but hid them from view. The hotels displayed an outward appearance of opulence and progression, but inside they clung to age-old biases. For the better part of the early 20th century, the Radisson topped the downtown Minneapolis skyline. A glass-and-iron canopy extended 50 feet from its marble columns and bronze doorways. The lobby boasted the finest candy, confections, and sodas. A cigar shop displayed humidors capable of storing a million cigars each. Yet when Dr. George Haynes, the executive secretary of the Department of Race Relations of the Federal Council of Churches checked in, he was asked to kindly take his meals in his room. While Black men were permitted to work in the hotel dining rooms, they were not allowed to eat there. Even as late as 1939, Duke Ellington's star trumpet player, Rex Stewart, was forced to take the freight elevator lest he be seen by other hotel guests. Black men who traveled to the hotel for a Young Republicans conference met the same "hospitality."

Of all the downtown hotels, the Curtis Hotel seemed to be held in somewhat higher regard by the local Black community. For many years, it was the only hotel to employ waiters of color. By 1940 the Curtis would be the de facto recommendation by Black railroad workers to Black train passengers arriving in Minneapolis. But though it may have been held in higher regard, it did not offer any semblance of equal treatment.

When the Cyclones football team sat down for dinner at the Curtis the night before their big game, Bob Fisher looked around. He looked up and down the table. "Where's Jack?" he asked his teammates. He couldn't believe what he was told: Jack couldn't dine with the team because he was Black.

Upstairs in his room, Jack sat at a small desk. Unable to eat with his teammates because of the color of his skin, his mind turned to greater things. His was no stranger to prejudice; after all, no Black man was. But the divide between him and those around him seemed to be widening. Maybe not physically but certainly culturally. Students would later recall Jack strolling through the south side of campus. He worked out in the gym. He attended convocation. He rubbed elbows with them. But he never stepped over "the invisible barrier." He "lived alone and apart." Like his high school yearbook, the college newspaper commented on his smile. Even the students on campus who didn't know him personally still experienced his smile. But to many, that was as close as they could get to Jack. It was true: There was a barrier. But it wasn't invisible. It was big and black. Jack worked for the greater good, to lift up those around him. He was an idealist.

With a weighted mind, he picked up a leaf of Curtis Hotel stationery that night. He put pen to paper, dated it October 5, 1923, and began to write:

To whom it may concern:
My thoughts just before the first real college game of my life. The honor of my race, family and self are at stake. Everyone is expecting me to do big things. I will!

My whole body and soul are to be thrown recklessly about on the field tomorrow. Every time the ball is snapped I will be trying to do more than my part. On all defensive plays I must break thru the opponents line and stop the play in their territory.

Beware of mass interference, fight low with your eyes open and toward the play. Roll block the interference. Watch out for cross bucks and reverse end runs. Be on your toes every minute if you expect to make good.

He signed the letter and looked over at the clock. It was 7:45 PM and time for the team meeting.

The next morning, excitement filled the air. Hundreds of fans had made the drive from Iowa to Minneapolis to catch the game. The rest stayed behind in Ames and filled the State Gymnasium. For the price of a quarter, they could follow the game on a Grid-Graph. A miniature football field showed the players' positions, who had the ball, and the type of play. Announcements were made as updates came over the telegraph from Minnesota. All the players' names lined the side of the board. When a person made a play, his name would light up. Along the top of the board ran the quarter and yardage information. Cora was among those in attendance at the gym, eagerly waiting to hear how Jack and the East Tech boys did in their new adventure.

More than 12,000 fans awaited the two teams' appearance on Northrup Field. It was a crisp and clear day, and the student stands filled up well before the game. University of Minnesota cheerleaders riled up the crowd, leading them in Gophers chants (it was the first year women were allowed on the cheer squad).

*Minnesota, hats off to thee,*
*To thy colors true we shall ever be.*
*Firm and strong, united are we.*
*Rah, rah, rah, for Ski-U-Ma!*

Willaman waited with his team for the signal to run onto the field. With the crowd roaring behind him, he turned to the team. He reminded them of the challenge ahead. This was a big game against a larger and more experienced team. But he knew they were going to give all they had. It was their determination that would be their edge. His eyes moved toward Jack's. "Boys," he said, "I know of two men on this team I know will fight." He let everyone know Jack Trice was one of them. At 2:00 PM, the Cyclones ran onto the field and began warming up. The Iowa State fans on the south end of the field threw their hands and voices high into the air above them. The cheerleaders bellowed in megaphones:

*A-m-e-s Rah! Rah!*
*A-m-e-s Rah! Rah!*
*Hoo-Rah! Roo-Ray!*
*State College-Ioway!*

Then they pointed above the crowd for the Sky Rocket yell:

*Z-z-z-z-z-z Boom!!! Ah!*
*AMES!!!!*

Seconds later, the Locomotive chant rumbled through the Cyclones' corner:

*A-m-e-s Rah! Rah! Rah! Rah!*
*A-m-e-s Rah! Rah! Rah! Rah!*
*A-m-e-s Rah! Rah! Rah! Rah!*
*Ames! Ames! Ames!*

At 2:17 PM the Minnesota Gophers materialized on the sideline. The maroon mass emerged onto the field, breaking up into smaller groups. One squad practiced kicking and punting, and another worked on passing. Team captain and All-American Earl Martineau showed up with his broken right hand wrapped for protection. He wasn't expected to play that day. Showing he could still kick the ball, he pleaded to Spaulding over the din of the crowd to let him play. The Minnesota coach just shook his head and directed him to the bench. They were going to play without him.

Finally, at 2:30 PM the starters lined up. Gold on one side, maroon on the other. And green clover beneath their feet. Jack looked across the field. With only leather helmets for protection, you could see every part of your opponent's face, and they yours. Minnesota had won the coin toss and elected to kick the ball. Norty received the opening kickoff and returned it for 15 yards. Iowa gained another three yards on a short run. A quick pass to Norty was stuffed as Minnesota tackled him for a seven-yard loss. The Minnesota team was holding the Cyclones players close and keeping the game physical. The next play led to another loss of yardage. Iowa fumbled the snap for a punt and the Gophers broke through the line. With the Cyclones staggering backward, Minnesota recovered the fumble on Ames's 4-yard line. Two plays later, the home team scored the first touchdown of the game, sending the crowd into a frenzy and the Cyclones to the benches for discussion.

Jack walked back to the sideline holding his left shoulder. He had felt something crack or pop near his collarbone. Perhaps it was broken. Another possibility was that he had separated the small joint where the collarbone meets the top of the shoulder blade—a common football injury called an AC separation, and maybe a little easier to play through. According to the rules of the day, if Jack went out then, he couldn't return until the second half. So he didn't say anything; he just held his shoulder.

The team regrouped and returned to the field. Only four minutes had passed, and the rest of the game lay ahead. They needed to focus on their strategy: aerial passes, quick runs, and strong interference. Johnny received the kick on the 10-yard line and returned it for almost 40 yards before being forced out of bounds. Ames, however, couldn't capitalize. Minnesota regained the ball on downs, but this time the Cyclones' defensive line held their own. The first quarter ended with the Gophers up 7–0.

The second quarter saw Iowa State looking more like the "flashy" team they were expected to be. The Cyclones sent more and more passes into the air. The Gophers defenders were often caught off guard, leaving them dizzy from nearly 70 yards of passing plays. Johnny received a pair of passes. Then Norty caught his own for a 30-yard gain, bringing the ball to Minnesota's 5-yard line. With fourth down and inches left, Ames went for the touchdown and carried the ball over the goal line. The first half ended with the game tied 7–7.

During halftime, Willaman asked Jack if he was all right. Jack reassured him he was. Spaulding, meanwhile, was beginning to panic. The second quarter had shown Minnesota's weakness against the passing game. The game looked like it could go either way. He went over to Martineau. He was going into the game. His hand was bandaged, so he couldn't pass, but he could run. Spaulding wanted him in as halfback.

The second half started with Iowa State kicking the ball. When the crowd saw Martineau take the field, their dampened spirits livened back up. His presence on the field seemed to inspire everyone, his own teammates included. This was going to be the year they won the Big Ten championship, and they weren't going to let the farmers from Iowa stand in their way. Ames was able to hold Minnesota's offense and relied on passes to the Behm brothers for their own offense. But with Ames deep into their own territory, Minnesota's right tackle Louis Gross swatted a pass down and it deflected into the hands of one of his own players, who ran the intercepted pass back for a touchdown. The Gophers regained the lead 14–7.

Johnny received the kick again and returned it for nearly 20 yards. Norty received a pass but was tackled for a loss. The next play, Johnny ran to get open. Out of the corner of his eye his saw Jack running forward to help make room for him. As usual, Jack had been able to make holes for him by overpowering his man. But this time, instead of locking up, Jack just dropped. It looked like the other guy had tackled him to the ground. Johnny grabbed the pass as it whizzed by and ran for 25 yards before being downed by Martineau. He got up and started to walk back to his team, when he spotted a small crowd across the field. Several Minnesota players were getting up, but someone was still lying on the ground. It was Jack.

Sometimes Jack did a "roll block," where he took a few opposing players down with him, but this looked different. Jack was on his back, his body exposed. It was a straight power play, Johnny thought to himself. Clearly the opposing end had been tired of being beaten and taken Jack out of the play the only way he could—illegally. The fullback must have stepped on him once he was down. Louis Gross, who lined up opposite Jack, recalled three or more players ran over Jack, but to him, it looked like an accident. At first no one thought Jack was seriously hurt. Later accounts would reverse the original flow of the play and have Jack on defense running from the other side of the field to help stop the play. In both scenarios, his abdomen was trampled by several Minnesota players.

The call went across the telegraph: Trice was down. Back in Ames, the world slowed down around Cora. Jack was hurt. She held her head and her breath. She could feel the eyes in the room on her. Jack struggled to get up to a sitting position, insisting he was all right. Cyclones Ira Young and Harry Schmidt helped Jack to his feet. It was announced across the wire that Jack was walking off the field. Cora breathed a sigh of relief and looked back up, her gaze trained on the Grid-Graph.

Shortly after Jack left the field supported by his two teammates, Iowa State kicked a 37-yard field goal to bring the game within four points. The scoreboard on the field and the Grid-Graph in Ames clicked to 14–10. Ames was back in the game. The following minutes of the fourth quarter kept both teams' fans on their feet. First, Minnesota fans erupted in cheers when their team scored a touchdown, but then they groaned when they failed to make the field goal for the extra point. A few minutes later, the Cyclones' section exploded when Johnny intercepted a pass and ran 80 yards for a touchdown. The game continued in a tense back-and-forth. Defensive stops capped both teams' efforts. The final seconds of the game clock ticked down. Soon the whistles sounded and the announcement went across the Iowa State gymnasium. The Gophers had held on to their lead, winning the game 20–17. The consequences were quickly realized: The game would have been a major stepping-stone for Willaman and Iowa State in college football's echelon. It was a particularly painful loss.

Meanwhile, Jack had been taken to University Hospital. He was initially evaluated on the sideline by Ames' trainer, Dr. Benjamin Dvorak. Dvorak was a physician and former Minnesota football player. What he saw unfolding concerned him. Jack's condition seemed more serious than just some bruising from a football scuffle. They were joined by Iowa State's athletic director and Minnesota's assistant director of physical education (and Gophers basketball coach), Dr. L.J. Cooke. Jack lay on the examination table while the three doctors conferred. They considered keeping him overnight for observation, but Jack protested. He wanted to go home with his team. He wanted to see Cora.

After a series of hushed back-and-forths, the doctors agreed to let Jack take the train home with his team. He arrived in time to be placed onto a mattress made of straw. During the long journey back to Iowa, his teammates looked over him. Each bump on the journey seemed to bring Jack worsening pain. Once the train arrived, Jack was separated from his team and rushed to the Iowa State campus hospital. At first it seemed things were improving, but then his breathing became more shallow and labored. His neck muscles began to tighten as he struggled to deliver oxygen to the rest of his body. His abdomen became rigid and fixed. The doctors at the hospital quickly phoned Des Moines and requested to speak to Dr. Oliver Fay, a renowned stomach specialist. Fay quickly rushed to the train station, arriving at the hospital late in the night. He examined Jack as the young football player lay in the metallic hospital bed, white sheets scattered around him.

Fay pushed his fingers down into Jack's tense abdomen. The young man squirmed in discomfort. Then Fay pulled his hands back up into the air. The release of pressure caused Jack even more discomfort. The painful rebounding of his abdominal wall signaled a worsening prognosis: peritonitis. The lining of Jack's abdominal cavity had become inflamed. Either due to bleeding or infection from a ruptured bowel, his injury was no longer isolated to one organ. It had begun to invade the surrounding structures. This was much more serious than just a football injury; this was life-threatening, high-level trauma.

Fay discussed the situation with the school's doctors. Peritonitis was a dangerous condition. An operation could be performed, but there were great risks involved. It had already spread. His intestines had already stopped moving. The sounds of his bowels were now silent. Surgically, Fay could open up the intestines to relieve pressure and close them back up again, but Jack likely would not survive. They could place drains in various parts of the abdomen to decompress it, but this would only treat a small area of what looked like a much bigger problem. The process was already too advanced. The only thing left was to give him antibiotics and hope his body could fight off the infection. Sunday came to a close and Monday arrived. Jack continued to deteriorate.

By Monday afternoon, Jack struggled to open his eyes. Jack's fraternity brother Harold Tutt rushed to the campus cafeteria to find Cora staring at her food. She had to return quickly. Cora arrived back at Jack's bedside. "Hello, darling," she said, looking down on him. Jack's eyes faintly rose to meet hers, but he could not speak. Outside the windows of his room, the Campanile bells chimed 3:00 across the campus. By the time the last bell tolled, Jack had stopped breathing. Cora froze, clutching the necklace Jack had given to her. It was all she had left of him. She began to wail. It was October 8, 1923. Jack was gone.

# 10

## "I Go Higher"

WORD OF JACK'S DEATH RIPPLED ACROSS THE CAMPUS. FOOTBALL practice was canceled. Jack's mother was phoned in Ravenna. Lee and Pearl were contacted in Cleveland. Meanwhile, Jack's personal effects were gathered to bring to Cora. As his jacket was folded up, a small piece of stationery fell out of its pocket. "To whom it may concern" was written across its top.

Two days later, the school canceled classes at 3:00 PM for Jack's memorial service, at which 3,000 students gathered in a large semicircle around the Campanile. A large wooden platform rose above a gray casket. A cardinal-and-gold Ames blanket rested atop the coffin. Following the invocation and a song, President Pearson strode to the podium. The eyes of the crowd were fixed on him. Pearson spoke about Jack and his accomplishments. Then slowly he unfolded a piece of paper before him. It was the letter that was found in Jack's coat pocket. With Cora's permission, Pearson said, he would like to read it aloud. Jack's words reverberated off the northwest corner of the Campanile. Pearson announced that to honor him and his words, Jack's letter would forever be preserved in the college archives.

During the funeral service, several other administration officials gave their solemn words of condolence to Cora and Jack's mother. Anna had arrived the evening before with Lee, who sat beside her. According to Pearson, each person she encountered felt both her composure and her strength. Ira Young spoke for Jack's teammates. The chaplain announced a fund would be created in honor of Jack.

The somber ceremony came to a close with a performance of "Nearer My God to Thee." It was a Christian hymn that told the story of Jacob's dream in the book of Genesis. As Jacob dreamed, a ladder was set upon earth. Its top reached up to heaven. There angels were ascending and descending along its length. It was to this tune of arrival and departure from our world that Jack's casket was carried away. Six of his teammates stood by his side as pallbearers, including Johnny, Norty, Spike, and Harry Schmidt.

Cora and Anna returned home with Jack's body. They were joined by Lee, Jack's fraternity brother Harold Tutt, and freshman football coach and minister William Thompson. Thompson offered words of comfort to Jack's family, finding them to be "God-fearing" people. William Pew, the former Iowa State dean and Cora's family friend, met the mourners at the station. He brought them to his family home in Ravenna, the one Cora and her father had known so well.

Cora was devastated and appeared physically unwell. A local doctor was called to the house to examine her and reassured everyone she just needed to rest. The funeral party spent the night in Ravenna before traveling the final leg to Hiram. There, where Jack had begun his life's journey, he was laid to rest near his father. A funeral service was held for Jack. President Bates, Gaylord's father who had known both Jack and his father, spoke to the crowd. He remarked on the journey Jack had made, an unlikely path that had begun with all four of his grandparents forced into slavery.

Meanwhile in Ames, a letter written the day Jack died came across the desk of Samuel Beyer, Iowa State's first athletic director. He was considered the godfather of Cyclones sports and had deep relationships with the athletic officials at other schools. The letter, addressed to him by the University of Missouri's athletic director, read as follows:

Dear Professor Beyer:

We understand from newspaper reports that you have a colored man playing with your football squad this Fall. I am quite sure, Professor Beyer, you know conditions here, and know it is impossible for a colored man to play or even appear on the field with any team. This has been discussed in the Missouri Valley for a good many years and I know that you understand the tradition that a colored man cannot come here. This whole question is bigger than our athletics and there is no alternative for us other than to say that we cannot permit a colored man on any team that we play. I am writing your Mr. Otapolik also, because I did not want any misunderstanding or confusion late in the week. I hope to see you some time during the Fall and renew our friendship of the old days.

With sincere personal regards, I am very truly yours,

C. L. Brewer, Director

Sam Beyer responded on the day of Jack's funeral with the following reply:

Dear Mr. Brewer:

I have your good favor of recent date relative to the Saturday's game. It has been understood for several years by the faculty members of the schools in Iowa and Nebraska that colored men could not be used on teams playing with schools from the states of Missouri, Kansas and Oklahoma. There is no written rule on the subject, only a gentlemen's agreement. We had no intention of using Jack Trice in the game with you. However that is all settled because Jack's injury resulted in his death Monday afternoon. I am handing you herewith copy of letter Jack wrote the day before the game. From the letter one would not help feel that Jack must have had premonition of what actually happened. I am very glad on account of Missouri Valley that you have returned to the fold.

With kindest personal regards, I am yours cordially and sincerely,

SWB

Following Jack's funeral, Cora was unable to return to school as the grief of Jack's death continue to weigh on her. She moved in with Anna. Meanwhile Harold returned to school and arranged for a memorial service at 1125 Kellog Avenue, the Gater home. It was a common gathering place for members of the Black community in Ames. There, among other people of color, his fraternity brothers offered their own respects to Jack. Harold relayed the events of Jack's funeral in Ohio. L.A. Potts spoke on "Trice—the Student," while another brother gave a eulogy titled "Jack Trice: A Representative of Our Race." The owner of the house, Edwin Gater, read Jack's last letter to everyone in attendance. At the end of the service, a collection was made to help Anna and Cora with Jack's funeral expenses.

The students at Iowa State also carried out their own collection, soliciting donations from the downtown business district and Campustown. They set out milk jugs for donations. The money was used to help Anna pay off her mortgage and further alleviate Jack's funeral expenses. Jack's mother, it seemed, had mortgaged her house to help send Jack to school. The funds were dispatched to Pew in Ravenna. The Athletics Council also sent the family a varsity *A*. Jack never played in his third game, but his dedication was without question. He had earned it. Anna asked Cora if she could keep the badge of honor. To her, it had become something sacred.

Still struggling with her loss, Anna wrote to President Pearson, who passed her letter on to Willaman. In it she wrote: "If there is anything in the life of John Trice and his career that will be an inspiration to the colored students who come to Ames, he has not lived and died in vain. But Mr. President, while I am proud of his honors, he was all I had, and I am old and alone. The future is dreary and lonesome."

Anna, who had lost her husband and her son, shared a poem that had provided her solace. It was written by Jesse Brown Pounds, also a child born in Hiram:

## The Idealist

*He followed his dream and men counted it madness;*
*He followed his dream up the mountain's steep side;*
*"See! Here in the valley are music and gladness;*
*Why then take the highway, the hard way?" they cried.*
*At length from above them we heard a faint calling;*
*His scorners turned quickly from feasting and play,*
*To look toward the mountain height grim and appalling;*
*"The luck of a fool—he has treasure!" said they.*
*With ropes and with staves they toiled after, and found him*
*Midway of the mountain, his treasure outspread;*
*"Let us share it!" they clamored, pressed rudely around him;*
*"Take all—it is yours; I go higher," he said.*

Willaman and the team finished out their season. To honor Jack, they each wore black armbands. The black stripes adorned their uniforms during their next game against Missouri. It was the third game of the varsity season, after which the rest of the starters would earn their letters. It was also the game Jack would have been forbidden to play in due to a "gentleman's agreement."

News of Jack and his letter spread from coast to coast, and dispatches were run as far as Hawaii and Alaska. Articles were written and columns penned extolling the virtue of Jack's sacrifice. Some called him a national hero, others a martyr. Many more called him a credit to his race.

At the end of the 1923 season, the editor of the Iowa State College newspaper wrote, "Some tribute, some tangible thing, must be set up in memory of Jack Trice.... What form this tribute may best take cannot yet be known, but the thought and comment of a student body can determine it."

And the students did determine to honor Jack indefinitely. The Double-A varsity athletes solicited ideas. By December it was deemed that a plaque would be inscribed with the words of Jack's letter and placed on the walls of Iowa State's gym for all to see. "I will!" he had said of doing something great. The power of his letter spoke to people. His words were timeless. They would inspire students, athletes, and people for generations to come. His story was not over.

# Part 2
# The Handoff

*The revolution will not be televised.*

—GIL SCOTT-HERON,
"THE REVOLUTION WILL
NOT BE  TELEVISED"

# 11
# A Nutty-Violent Period

AMES IN THE 1960S WAS CONSIDERED A PEACEFUL PLACE. IT WAS THE kind of town where residents never locked their doors. They had heard about racial unrest in Des Moines, where groups such as the Black Panthers had set up shop. But nobody though a place like Ames would see any real violence, not like the two bombings in Des Moines or the one that would happen at Drake University in 1970. Those types of things didn't happen in small towns with Main Streets. And yet Iowa State's latest president, Robert Parks—appointed in 1965—had been trying for years to stamp out the smoldering embers of racial protest on campus.

Parks was born on a farm in Tennessee in 1915, less than three hours by car from the birthplace of Jack's father, Greene. Parks was two generations removed from Tennessee slave owners and the Confederacy. But he didn't let his ancestry define him, geographically or politically. He purposely sought his PhD in political science at the progressive University of Wisconsin.

He stood six feet tall and moved with the physical agility of a lifelong athlete. He could still dunk a basketball well into his sixties.

Gifted not only with physical agility but also political agility, Parks was described by those around him as a savvy leader. At Iowa State, he became known as a strong negotiator. By softening the sharp edges of his rigid work ethic and strong opinions with a dry humor, he skillfully managed to work his way up the academic state-school bureaucracy.

By the time Parks joined the faculty of Iowa State as dean of instruction in 1958, the power that lay in naming something was a subject of considerable debate. For decades, Iowa State College had struggled to define itself beyond being called just Ames. In 1958 the school was faced with the decision to change its name from Iowa State College to Iowa State University. As a new faculty member, Parks quickly found himself pushing for the name change. In the process, he became the primary author of the official name-change recommendation and established himself as an important political conduit between the powerful board of regents, who often had the final word on state school–related matters, and the interests of the university.

During his journey from childhood in the South to pursuing a liberal political education in Madison, Wisconsin, Parks came to believe racial progress was a balancing act. Change happened in tempered and measured steps. When Parks first arrived at Iowa State, less than 1 percent of the university community identified as Black. By the 1960s there were still fewer than 100 Black students out of a university population of 12,000. There were only 29 Black families in the whole town.

In 1963, two years before Parks became university president, he established an advisory committee on racial relations. He tapped William Murray, a former Republican candidate for governor, to lead the Human Relations Committee. Park understood the need to improve racial relations, but at the same time, he reportedly didn't want a "wild-eyed liberal leading it." Many of the male student-athletes told the committee they had been reluctant to attend Iowa State University because there were only a handful of Black men and even fewer Black women on campus. It was clear the university had a diversity problem.

In 1968 Parks created Iowa State's first director of minority affairs position when he hired William Bell. "Big Bill" Bell was Ohio State's first Black football player in 33 years, and third overall, after Frederick Patterson (who was of mixed race) in 1891 and Julius Tyler in 1896. Bell first broke the racial barrier at the Willaman brothers' alma mater in 1929 and then established a long career as a successful football coach and athletic director for Historically Black Colleges and Universities. Parks and Bell began to lay the foundation for what would become Iowa State University's Black Cultural Center. The catalyst for Parks's increased efforts emerged in the wake of Martin Luther King Jr.'s assassination that same year.

The day after Dr. King fatally stepped out onto the balcony of Room 306 of the Lorraine Motel in Memphis, approximately 40 Black Iowa State students marched into the Memorial Union. It was shortly after noon, and most of the students on campus had gathered there to eat lunch. The solemn, stony-faced group entered the commons wearing dark suits. They moved as a unit, filling their trays with glasses of water and orange juice. A disturbing screech of friction rang out as they pushed several large lunch tables together. They sat down without saying a word, staring ahead into space. Sensing the tension in the air, the other students got up from their seats and backed away from their half-eaten food, ceding the space. Then, in unison, the Black students stood up, lifting their glasses into the air, and made a toast. "To Black unity on campus!" their leader shouted. The group responded by throwing their glasses to the floor. The glasses smashed into pieces. Then without saying another word, they flipped over their tables and chairs and defiantly marched out across the shards of broken glass. The remaining White students stood in place, shocked at what had just transpired. For a minute, no one spoke or moved. Then, as the workers moved in to clean up the debris, a male student asked out loud, "What was the purpose of all this? What did they expect to accomplish?" The answer came from a female student nearby: "You ask what they do this for? That's what is wrong with all of us!"

Following the Memorial Union protest, and under the direction of several Black-militant Iowa State University students, a statement was issued: "We, the Black students of Iowa State University, are here to awaken *you* to the conditions and consequences of the situation which led to the violent death of our nonviolent leader, the Most Reverent Dr. Martin Luther King Jr." The student leaders warned President Parks and the university that the students' reaction could have been much worse. They had spared them what they deserved. One student in particular, Roosevelt Roby, warned the school that it "got off lucky." He said the students in the cafeteria "could have torn up the whole Union." They also unveiled a formally adopted a constitution, establishing Iowa State University's first Black Student Organization.

The first official act of the BSO became known as the Eight Grievances. The Eight Grievances highlighted the racism and marginalization felt by members of the BSO and was written on behalf of the Black athletes of Iowa State. The first three demands were: 1) There should be a Black coach in each major sport at Iowa State. 2) There should be Black personnel in the athletic administration at Iowa State. 3) Prejudice and despotism of the coaches between Black and White athletes should be stopped immediately. Performance, attitude, and desire to play should be the prevailing factors.

The remaining grievances were: 4) The school's athletic trainer should be removed from his position or forced to change his general attitude, especially with reference to his treatment of injured Black athletes. 5) Student-athletes should be given more leeway in class attendance during the season. 6) Athletes should be given preferential treatment in deciding where they got to live. 7) Athletes, especially Black athletes, should be allowed to work while on scholarship given their poor financial backgrounds. 8) Black students were to be referred to as Afro-American or Black; the word "Negro" would no longer be tolerated.

If these grievances were not addressed, the Black student-athletes would leave Iowa State in protest. The administration and President Parks made some attempts to placate the demands, but the BSO found their efforts unsatisfactory. Several of the athletes, and the president of the BSO, kept their word and left Iowa State University. Parks suffered a political black eye. He was reminded by a powerful local politician that images have consequences. "Every disruptive act harms the university," state senator Francis Messerly informed him. He continued, "I have over and over again stressed that the universities must present a better image or that the taxpayers will not support the schools." He then pointed out the piles of letters he had been receiving demanding stronger leadership from Iowa State University administrators.

From 1966 to 1975, the environment at ISU was described as a "nutty-violent period" by Iowa State journalism professor and student newspaper adviser Bill Kunerth. Smack in the middle of this time period, a purported racial conflict really brought things to a head. On April 10, 1970, a group of White Iowa State University wrestlers were gathered at the Red Ram, a popular tavern in downtown Ames. The ISU wrestling team had just won its second of back-to-back NCAA national championships. Located across the bar from the group of White wrestlers was a group of Black students, including Roosevelt Roby, who had already issued his aforementioned warning to Parks and Iowa State University. Stewing next to his beer, Roby exchanged some words with the wrestlers. Rumors were the White wrestlers and Black students had not gotten along for some time. The two groups stood up and faced off. A few of them shoved each other. Then, two-time NCAA wrestling champion Chuck Jean struck Roosevelt Roby in the throat. Roby retaliated by grabbing a nearby beer mug and hit Jean in the head with it. A melee ensued, with wrestlers and students fighting each other with what they had available. Someone called the police, who quickly arrived and broke up the two groups. They dragged the combatants outside the bar, where the crowd quickly grew. In the center of it, Roby could be seen yelling profanities at both the athletes and the police. Nevertheless, Roby's fight against the White wrestlers found sympathy among many supporters, including the *Daily*. Two days after the fight, the school paper ran an editorial featuring a picture of six Black students holding a gloved Black Power salute above their heads during a recent Iowa State football game. Underneath the picture, the headline read, RIGHT ON!

The ugly incident hung over the campus like a thick, suffocating blanket. Jean, one of the country's top wrestlers, was charged with disturbing the peace and soon dismissed from the wrestling team. About a week after the fight, detectives showed up on campus outside Roby's dorm. They spotted him just as he was leaving the building. They called out to him that they just wanted to talk. Roby and his friends ignored them and kept walking. A patrol car a few blocks away intercepted the group. The officers got out of the car and pulled Roby aside. They served him with a warrant for assault and battery. They tried to put the young Black militant into the patrol car, but Roby refused to go with them. The officers decided they needed to restrain Roby and put him in handcuffs.

By this point, a crowd of Black students had begun to grow around the officers, cutting them off from their car. As the officers' attention was turned to the growing chaos around them, Roby broke free. He took off, running deep onto campus and into one of its buildings. The police pursued him, but Roby got away. For an entire day, cars and officers searched the campus. They labeled Roby a fugitive. Eventually, with the help of Wilbur Layton, vice president for student affairs, and "Big Bill" Bell, Roby agreed to come out of hiding and turn himself in.

Two weeks later, amidst a rising sea of tension, Roby had his criminal hearing at the Ames courthouse downtown. Black protesters crowded the steps of the courthouse shouting their support for Roby. Some held signs that read FREE ROBY and THERE IS NO JUSTICE FOR THE BLACK MAN IN AMES. As the crowd swelled, it began to overwhelm the few officers on duty and push them back onto the steps. Backup was called in, and a mixed bag of additional police officers, highway patrolmen, deputy sheriffs, and other law enforcement officials arrived to secure the situation. When the judge for the case, John L. McKinney, finally arrived, one protester blocked his path. McKinney ordered the protester to move, and when the man stood defiantly in his path, the judge ordered a nearby officer to arrest him.

Once inside the building, McKinney donned his robe and entered the courtroom. Bailiff Herb Carr announced to everyone that court was in session and instructed them to rise. Hardly anyone moved. Carr announced it again. No one stirred. The judge looked around at what was unfolding and sternly ordered the courtroom cleared as he left the bench. The bailiff rebuked those in the audience that rising when the judge entered the courtroom was a mark of respect for the court. They needed to comply or face consequences. Gradually all those in the audience rose to standing. The judge reentered the courtroom and the hearing began. Lawyers argued and witnesses were called. One of the wrestlers argued from the stand that Roby had started the fight. Hearing this, Roby, who was sitting across from him at a table, yelled out in the courtroom that he was a liar. He started to stand, but his lawyer held on to his arm. Roby yelled at the wrestler, "If you're looking for a fight, I'll fight you!"

The hearing resumed the next day and stretched into the evening. After the hearing wrapped up, the judge drove back home. He was going to celebrate his 39th birthday with his family and an outdoor barbecue. Afterward McKinney, still feeling the pleasant aftereffects of the dinner, put his children to bed and brought their toys outside to the garage. Suddenly he stopped in his tracks. He was shaken to his core by what he saw. Waiting for him inside his garage was a homemade bomb. A one-gallon container with chemicals was wired to a travel alarm clock and a dry-cell battery. He quickly ran inside, where his wife was doing the dishes, and called the police. He then grabbed his wife and four children and fled to a neighbor's house.

Several Ames police officers arrived and inspected the device. It looked real to them. They called for a bomb-disposal expert, but the closest one was in Omaha. They decided they would place the device in a trash can and carry it to a nearby vacant field. As they went to place the bomb into the trash can, they noted the clock started ticking as soon as they moved it. They quickly placed it in the field and ran back to the rest of the officers as one of them shot the can with a .22 rifle. Nothing happened. The officers slowly approached the device and dismantled the battery connection, leaving it inert. Later analysis revealed it could very well have exploded.

By this time, word had spread of the bomb and news crews had shown up to McKinney's neighbor's house. Standing in the driveway, furious with emotion, the judge told the local reporters he was certain "the Blacks are behind this," adding, "I have no fear of the whites." Once he had calmed down, the judge commented bitterly, "The administration at Iowa State University is one of the prime causes. They shove their problems down to the city." The judge soon recused himself from the case.

During the time of Roby's trial, his friend Charles Knox was also facing charges. Knox had defended Roby when the police tried to arrest him. He demanded they release Roby, and when they refused, he shoved the police away from him. As a result, Knox became a codefendant in the Roby case. He was soon outed as the leader of the Black Panthers in Des Moines. For weeks Knox had been seen around the Iowa State campus, often with one of his roommates in tow, a 19-year old named James W. Lawson Jr. Lawson, it later turned out, was a suspected bomb maker.

Three weeks after Roby's case concluded in a mistrial, an explosion erupted inside city hall. It happened a little after 9:00 AM on May 22, 1970, just as downtown businesses were beginning to open up. The explosion shattered nearly all of the government building's windows. It tore into the bars of the jail, sending metal shrapnel into the throat of a prisoner. The impact radius was felt for nearly 20 blocks. Thirteen people were injured and one officer lost an eye. In a town where no one locked their doors, blood mixed with glass just two blocks from Main Street.

THREE WEEKS BEFORE the bombing in downtown Ames, Parks, and Iowa State University officials were busy furiously working to contain another powder keg. Anti–Vietnam War protests were being staged across the country, and Iowa State was no different. Like other university presidents, Parks was trying to keep the Black racial justice movement from combining with the Vietnam War protests. If the two waves combined, the school would be overwhelmed under a tsunami of unrest.

On May 4, 1970, just two days before the VEISHEA, National Guardsmen at Kent State University shot and killed four unarmed student protesters and wounded nine others. A significant number of universities across the country shut down in an effort to prevent further violence. Iowa State, however, remained open for its spring celebration. On May 6, the first day of the VEISHEA, the students began their own Vietnam demonstrations. More than 3,000 Iowa State students spread across campus. Some of them disrupted an ROTC drill, and others sat in the street, blocking traffic. From there many of them marched to the Selective Services building and entered it, shouting slogans of protest. At least two dozen demonstrators stayed inside for an all-night sit-in.

Giving them until the next morning to leave, the police arrived and ordered the students out of the building. If they refused, they were warned, tear gas would be used. Administrators from the Dean of Students Office arrived but failed to persuade the protesters to leave. The police ordered everyone out and began opening large tear gas canisters. The toxic smoke filled the building. A few moments went by before the demonstrators "came stumbling and coughing out into the bright sunshine." Several of them struggled with the waiting police officer and were forced to the ground, where their hands were cuffed behind their backs.

It was now the second day of the VEISHEA, and the annual parade was less than 24 hours away. Many questioned whether the event should still go on as planned. Concern grew that the parade would become a lightning rod for violence, an actual battleground. Rumors of "agitators" arriving by bus spread throughout Beardshear Hall. Word of a local armory break-in had also reached the university's center of operations that had been set up in the administrative building. There was talk of student protesters trying to take over the military building. Meanwhile, the highway patrol had amassed itself just outside of town. Carl Hamilton, one of Parks's closest and most trusted aides, flitted in and out of the room with updates. He was clearly disturbed by what he was hearing on the phone.

Parks continued walking an administrative tightrope. He made a point to listen more than he spoke. He attempted to balance the concerns of marching protesters with the traditions and interests of the school and town. His philosophy as president was that a university should be "concerned with deep human problems" but that at all costs things must remain peaceful. It was suggested that the National Guard be brought in, but Parks insisted the university could handle its own issues. Over the next few hours, several compromises were made designed to vent some of the steam that had built up. Traditionally, the military units in the parade would carry rifles. Instead all forms of weapons would be banned from display. A section of the parade would also be dedicated as a March of Concern for antiwar protesters. This was to be followed by 24 hours of an open microphone situated in central campus.

That afternoon, 5,000 students and faculty members marched in the March of Concern section of the parade, many of them with signs. A few trailed along on motorcycles. Many of the spectators lined up along Main Street expected to see long-haired hippies marching but instead saw largely White middle-class men and women. The imagery was very different from years before, when floats of flowers and colors marked the rite of spring. It was a very different atmosphere than the one in which Jack had stood. A few rogue protesters took to painting messages on sidewalks and buildings. Others tried to glue the doors of university buildings shut. The fountain outside the Memorial Union was filled with food coloring. A few windows were broken. But mostly things remained peaceful.

Following the parade, most of the 5,000 marchers gathered in the center of campus, where Parks addressed them, saying, "Bringing peace is the most important problem facing us. As president, I want to say you are going about it in the right way.... If the university is not concerned with deep human problems such as bringing peace, then what should it be concerned with?" Parks's words were well received. The marchers in attendance gave him a standing ovation. He had successfully navigated the minefield. The students wanted to be heard, and he gave them a megaphone. But an even larger balancing act awaited him.

IN THE FALL of 1973, Charles Sohn and Alan Beals were sitting across from each other sipping coffee. A chessboard lay between them. The two of them often met in the evening at Beals's apartment for coffee and chess. They were on the verge of another game when Alan paused for a moment. There was something he had been waiting to tell his old friend—something that had struck him deeply.

The pair had rekindled their decade-long childhood friendship when Alan came to ISU as an academic tutor for the school's athletes years later. The two men had grown up in Harlan, Iowa, and spent their teenage years together. Harlan was a predominantly White Iowa town. Sohn never recalled witnessing a racist statement or action growing up. The dominant lessons that Harlan gave their young were simple: Help others. Be good people.

When they were teenagers in the summer of 1958, the two of them planned a weeklong vacation before Sohn started his senior year at Harlan High and Beals left for Southern Methodist University. They drove to Hot Springs, Arkansas, where Sohn's aunt and uncle lived. They weren't there to relax or blow off some steam. The ideas of righteousness and justice had embedded themselves in their everyday psyche. The civil rights struggle was often at the forefront of their minds. So they drove to Arkansas on a pilgrimage. They wanted to visit Little Rock Central High School. There, less than a year earlier, Governor Orval Faubus had stood in front of the building expressly to bar the Little Rock Nine from desegregating the school.

On a bright weekday in July 1958, Charles and Alan parked their car at the foot of a large, grassy slope that led up to the imposing school building. They climbed the five sets of stairs up to the entrance, turned, and stood side by side, staring out over the immense and deserted scene. As Sohn recalled, they did not say much of anything at all. They simply cursed under their collective breath that racism had become so entrenched there. They didn't know it yet, but they would lend a hand in their own school-wide referendum. They descended back down the steps to their car, knowing that even for a brief moment in time, they had gained some sense of resolve.

That fall, Beals spent less than a semester at SMU before transferring to Iowa State. A campus cross burning triggered his return back home to Iowa. Sohn joined him in Ames the following year, where he studied English. Sohn would graduate in May 1963 and be hired by the English department in June 1964. He taught freshman English to classes he intentionally composed to be 50 percent Black and non-Black students and 50 percent male and female students. He also began serving as the faculty adviser to the Iowa State University Black

Culture Center. Beals, meanwhile, was focusing most of his tutoring efforts on serving Black athletes.

To say their intentions were primarily motivated by liberal guilt would be considered an overstatement, according to Sohn. He had qualms about not heading into the racist and dangerous South to join the Selma march, for example. He had a marriage to consider, and he tried to do what he could to humanize his classroom and Iowa State University. One vivid memory that stayed with him for decades occurred while attending the protest concert of Sweet Honey in the Rock. He and Beals locked arms in the balcony of Curtiss Hall as the all-woman African American ensemble captured the Harlan boys' hearts with their a cappella. The two of them swayed and cried, "We shall overcome someday." It was not Sohn and Beals's journey the women sang about, for it was not those two men who needed to overcome. But it was a cause that fueled them, and they wanted to help. It was a belief in the beauty that could be humanity.

So on that aforementioned evening, over chess and coffee, Beals recounted something that, unbeknownst to him and Sohn, would lay the foundation for a decades-long movement. He described to Sohn how he had come across an old, dusty plaque in State Gym. No one else seemed to notice it. In fact, he wasn't sure why he hadn't noticed it before. But there it was, behind a staircase. It was the last letter Jack Trice had written. From the plaque, Jack's words seemed to call to him. They echoed through time: "The honor of my race, family and self are at stake. Everyone is expecting me to do big things. I *will*!"

Both intrigued and inspired by Jack's words, Beals had gone to the library to learn more about Jack. He opened up the special collections box but was shocked to find a sparse offering. Most of the items in the collection were newspaper clippings from 1923 about Jack's death. But there was something else there that caught his eye. One other person had stumbled upon Jack's story in 1957 and had written about it.

Tom Emmerson had been a graduate student looking to get out of his physical education requirement and had convinced Harry Schmidt, then the director of physical education, to let him write about Iowa State University athletics for credit. Emmerson had discovered the plaque while waiting outside Schmidt's office and asked him about it. Schmidt happened to have been Jack's teammate and told Emmerson about Jack, his character, his breaking of barriers, and his ultimate sacrifice. Emmerson dug deep into the school's archives and published an article about Jack in the *Iowa State Scientist*, only to have Jack's story forgotten once more. Emmerson became a faculty member at Iowa State University, but no one else took an interest in Jack's story and his memory faded yet again.

Hearing Jack's story, Sohn was immediately hooked. He and Beals believed the story deserved to be told again. They shared a realization and excitement that there was something really important in it. With homecoming approaching, the timing for an article in the school paper couldn't be better. It would be the 50th anniversary of Jack's passing, and his sacrifice should be honored.

Alan sought out the student editor of the school newspaper, Jim Smith, who immediately liked the idea. What resonated most with Smith was the aspect of Jack's story that focused on bettering himself through education. Smith was one of the few African Americans at Iowa State who were not there on an athletic scholarship. He was on an academic scholarship and had chosen Iowa State as a stepping-stone for his career in journalism. Iowa State was known as an engineering school, but they wanted their engineers to publish, so the school had built a strong English and journalism department.

On October 5, 1973, the day before the homecoming football game, a game-changing article about Jack was published in the *Iowa State Daily*. It featured a picture of Jack in his football uniform as well as the plaque on the wall of the gym. The headline read: TRICE: A FORGOTTEN STORY REMEMBERED. After reading the article again, Sohn realized Jack's biography would be an ideal project for his freshman English class. There was still so much to learn about Jack and what had brought him to Iowa State.

Sohn shared Jack's story with his students. They immediately became interested in a project about Jack. They broke up into small research and writing groups. Some would focus exclusively on Jack's life, others on early athletics at Iowa State, and the remaining would highlight institutional racism. The groups contacted local libraries and set up interviews, and several students tried to track down any of Jack's acquaintances and relatives who might still be alive 50 years later. They reached out to the Ravenna Area Historical Society. Gaylord Bates, Jack's childhood friend from Hiram; Herb Proctor; and a few of his other friends from Ravenna received word of the students' efforts and worked with the local historical society to connect with the students and record what they remembered of Jack.

At the time, Iowa State University was building a brand-new football stadium with an expected completion date in 1975, only two years away. During a small group meeting, one of the Black women in the class suggested the idea of naming it Jack Trice Stadium. It was something many of the other members had been quietly thinking as well. Everyone paused, and then one of the Black male students chimed in, "There is no way the establishment would honor some poor dead Black kid like that!" That was all they needed to hear. The students became excited about the prospect of challenging the establishment. The idea went from lively banter to an actionable plan when the students decided to form the Jack Trice Memorial Stadium Committee. The fight had officially begun.

AS THE SNOW melted across campus in 1974 and the flowers began to bloom, it once again became time to plan the VEISHEA. And once again, President Parks was dealing with student unrest. On May 17, 1974, Parks's tenets of new humanism and belief in slow, progressive steps would be tested yet again, this time in his own office. While he was away from the school, nearly two dozen minority students arrived with a list of demands. They requested to speak to President Parks immediately. His administrative assistant informed them he was out of the office, but their insistence only grew stronger. Unsure what to do with what appeared to her a dangerous mob, the assistant pressed the emergency panic button.

Vice president for student affairs Wilbur Layton arrived to help. The assistant informed Layton that the students were armed with guns, but Layton saw no sign of weapons. The group shoved a list of 20 demands toward him. He calmly informed them that Parks was out of the office. The group demanded to see for themselves and pushed their way forward. Layton stood in the doorway, blocking their entry, and as several of the women tried to push past him, a small scuffle ensued. Seeing him touch one of the women, one of the men in the crowd swung a concealed pipe toward Layton. Layton lost his balance and fell backward into the doorway. As the pipe smashed the wooden doorframe next to his head, the wood exploded, leaving sharp splinters that lacerated his scalp. The gash was deep and required stitches.

Rather than head to the hospital, Layton chose to stay on campus. Holding his bloodied head, he immediately went over to the student health center and was quickly stitched up. He then called his wife to bring him a clean shirt; his current one had bloodstains on it. Bandaged and cleaned up, he returned to Parks's office and continued his talk with the students, who were still there waiting to be heard. He ushered them into the president's wood-paneled conference room. By this time, Parks had also arrived. Not wishing to escalate things any further, Parks calmly sat down in the conference room and for several hours spoke with leaders of the group.

In the tense meeting, the Black students expressed their desire for greater minority student enrollment and the right to speak directly to the president when racial issues arose. The group also lambasted Ames residents, its police department, as well as Iowa State University faculty and students for their "prejudice and harassment." When the dust settled and the meeting concluded, Layton and other officials "got the message [that Ames] was not a very comfortable place for Blacks to live." In fact, it probably hadn't been for a long time; Black students had always struggled to be seen and heard.

Now, decades after Jack had died on campus, the student body of Iowa State was not only pushing for Black students to be seen and heard, but they wanted something even more audacious. They wanted something no other major university had done before. They wanted to name a major college football stadium after Jack Trice. The student movement to name the new stadium after Jack was gaining traction. Members of the Jack Trice Memorial Stadium Committee were going door to door to drum up support. Nearly everyone they spoke to backed the idea. Local papers began to receive letters to the editor in support of Jack. "Who could disagree?" asked one of the writers. The *Marshalltown Times Republican* in Iowa officially endorsed the idea.

It was essential to drum up support for the cause on campus. The student body seemed eager to exercise its activism and independence at the time, and the Jack Trice Memorial Stadium Committee thought the 1974 VEISHEA would be the perfect time to get their message out.

That year's VEISHEA was touted as both educational and entertaining. Talks from conservative William F. Buckley Jr. would be counterbalanced by musicals and concerts. The year before, Sonny and Cher had performed, and this year the planners had secured the Motown group the Spinners. They would perform their No. 1 R&B hits "I'll Be Around" and "Could It Be I'm Falling in Love."

The pageantry and color of the VEISHEA parade were to be designed around the theme "Great Mistakes of the Past." One mistake the Jack Trice Memorial Stadium Committee wasn't ready to celebrate was relegating Jack's story to history. Largely composed of English 105 students with a cause, the committee was motivated and directed by Charles Sohn. Some students, such as chairperson Pam Dee, reached out to A.R. Sicuro, managing editor of the *Record Courier* in Ravenna. Sohn himself went out to interview those who knew Jack and published their recollections. Others, including Bill Walsh, recorded interviews with Jack's old teammate Harry Schmidt.

Lonnie Coleman, one of the school's Black football players, told the *Iowa State Daily* in 1974, "Every football player who steps on the field puts himself in the same frame of mind as Trice did." He believed if the school named the stadium after Jack, it would be an inspiration to future players. "Think of the impact it would make on players being recruited," he implored.

Each document and newspaper clipping was copied and bound together into the *Jack Trice Scrapbook*. It both introduced Jack's story and contained a petition that could be sent back to the school in support of naming the future football stadium for Jack. A picture of Jack graced the cover next to the words, *The Story of a Man, an Ideal, and a Stadium Waiting to Be Named.* The cost was a one-dollar donation to the Jack Trice Memorial Scholarship Fund. The Jack Trice Memorial Stadium Committee set up a table at the VEISHEA to sell scrapbooks, hand out petitions, and spread their message of support for Jack. It was a message that seemed easier to deliver than it actually turned out to be.

One of the students working the table that day was Frederick McConico, the manager of the Black Student Center and one of the students who had stormed President Parks's office. It was his brother Tony who swung the lead pipe that day. Like many of his peers of color, he was fed up with feeling marginalized. Sometimes he thought the only thing people understood was violence. But on this day, he wasn't there to fight with his body but rather with an idea—the audacious idea that the football stadium on campus could be named for a Black man. McConico called out to passersby to buy a program, to help support their movement. Many of them pretended not to see him and kept walking.

"Someday," Frederick recalled in a guest opinion letter to the *Iowa State Daily* on October 19, 1974, "when I'm able to look back on the sad situation at Iowa State—when asked what is the most vivid memory of my college days, I shall think of the super-white, elite middle class, nonchalant, racist-ass people of the ISU communities."

No matter where he went, McConico couldn't shake the feeling of being watched, of being Black. "It is such an integral part of every setting, whether it's in the classroom, a shopping center, or a bar. Everywhere I go I feel dozens of blue eyes staring at me until I look into them—then they seldom look back."

Referencing Jack, McConico opined, "The fact that this man was Black may be insignificant, but the fact that he gave his life to break racial barriers in college football deserves a little more recognition than it has had to date."

He continued, "We may have sold 100 of the 48-page scrapbooks, many of which were purchased by other Black people. But there are dudes selling programs for one dollar each and their business is considerably better than ours. I actually had people with money in hand take it back when they saw the Black face on the cover."

McConico called attention to what seemed to be the true underlying belief system in place. It was what was said when people were in the comfort of their own home, away from the scales of public opinion: "So many of you think you're fair, concerned, democratic, and all that bullshit, yet you continue to watch injustices done to minorities and to teach your children to love thy neighbor, as long as he isn't a [N-word] or a Jew!"

McConico's letter in the *Iowa State Daily* did not go unnoticed. His words were heard, but perhaps his message didn't resonate with those he wanted to reach, those who only saw an angry Black man.

Two letters were printed in response to McConico's letter. "Maybe shelling out a dollar to get a story that has been printed several times already in the newspapers might not be the hottest item now on the market. Instead, you jump to the conclusion that we're all against having the stadium named after Trice and the Blacks must really be hated here at ISU," wrote the first White student.

Like most of the students, Black or not, that writer supported the stadium naming movement. But to him, optics were nuanced. And validation wouldn't be found on a nameplate. His letter continued, "My sentiments, and those of my friends, are that the stadium should be named after Jack Trice, but it is not a matter to get all hot and bothered about. If it is named after him, great! If it isn't, everyone is still going to recognize what a great man he was."

Perhaps the student should have stopped there, but he didn't. Perhaps he said what many other White people were thinking when they came upon McConico or other people of color who spoke out like he did. It was an opinion that someone comfortably in the White middle class could afford to feel, and even say. "I think that Mr. Trice would have been appalled at this anger," the student's letter continued. "He was obviously a man who worked hard to build himself up as a person and was not one to go around screaming at his white brothers for not giving him a chance. The Blacks today have many more opportunities to do their thing than they did back in Trice's time, and even though there is still prejudice, matters will not be getting any better if there is needless nitpicking such as this going on."

Another White student took even more ground out from the feet of Frederick and his brothers with his indifference, and he was not alone. The 1970s were a time of progress, but it was still only a little more than a hundred years since slavery. The shackles were broken, but the whip still endured; its tails were just finer. In a published letter to the editors, he began "Frederic Mconico and his five friends and other 'minority' students at ISU – please read this."

"In my opinion," the student continued, "the reason your book isn't selling, is that no one knows who Jack Trice is or what he did. Not everyone has money to give to a good cause, and even fewer have got money to waste on something they know nothing about."

His White privilege, unappreciated and likely unaware, came to the forefront at the conclusion of his letter. "Sometimes you've been treated wrong by blue eyes, but please avoid the attitudes of the '50s and '60s by classifying everyone by a few people's actions," he wrote. "I'm sure the world doesn't stop turning and everything quit just because you come into some place. If you back off and watch the people who were staring at you, they are probably staring at everyone who comes in," concluded the writer.

It wasn't just indifference that Jack's spirit still fought. It was also the administration. Despite petitions and student support, the administration turned a blind eye to the movement. To them it was a blip in the radar, a fleeting fancy of a student body looking for a cause. As Charles Sohn put it to the press in May 1974, "The only noticeable reluctance to support the name Jack Trice Stadium has been from university officials."

Sohn had succeeded in getting the library in the Black Cultural Center named after Jack. It became known as the Jack Trice Resource Center. But there seemed to be more losses than gains in the battle for Jack's legacy. The committee continued its efforts, but Sohn felt maybe the efforts themselves were coming under fire. As a result, the young English teacher informed the local paper he was disbanding the committee. It had become a focal point for Jack Trice retractors. It seemed maybe the committee was hurting its own cause—and Jack's—by speaking up so loudly. But there was someone else who was willing to stand up and be heard, someone else who was willing to sit across the table from the administration and be the voice of the student body. And that someone was also a woman.

JILL **WAGNER** STOOD at the podium of the Ames Ramada Inn and looked out over the sea of faces waiting for her to speak. It was the fall of 1975, and Jill was being inaugurated as the next president of the Iowa State University Government of the Student Body, known as the GSB. A certain sense of satisfaction came over her as she prepared to give her inaugural address. She was only 20 years old, but she knew the power of a platform. She also knew the importance of using that platform to help those without a voice. She had grown up in Colorado. Her mom was an activist and had marched for Cesar Chavez. Her parents took her out of their insulated, church-centric life and moved them closer to the inner city of Denver. Like Jack's mother, Jill's mom wanted her to experience a more diverse environment. In this case, to see how non-Whites and Hispanics lived and the problems they faced.

She straightened herself up, placed a hand on either side of the podium, took a deep breath, and began. "I am a woman." She paused. She let that settle in and then continued, "But it would be a denial of equality if my gender was the only novelty of this occasion."

Wagner continued, "The ordinary view of student government is that it has no power. This view is historically and pragmatically incorrect. Some of the first major universities in the modern era were founded in Paris and Bologna. These same universities were also shaped by the power of students."

She went on, "At that time, any student could ask for a poll of their class regarding the preparedness of the instructor. If a majority of students said that an instructor had not prepared for class, the instructor was not paid for that day."

Wagner said, "The faculty's response to student power was collective bargaining. A system of checks and balances between students and faculty. Unfortunately, student academic freedom has never been an established operating principle of American universities."

The words seemed to flow from deep inside her. She could taste the words as they left her mouth. "There can be no responsibilities without rights, and a university policy which imposes duty without rights is morally wrong and anti-educational," she posited.

Earlier in the evening, George Christensen, the vice president for academic affairs, had remarked, "Students are consumers, not managers, of a university. They have a right to work for improvement of the services they are buying."

He continued, "Students today have different priorities than students ten years ago. There is a marked trend in student awareness of the academic environment."

It had been four years since Congress lowered the voting age to 18 in 1971, and that moment in history was not lost on Wagner. Society was still shifting toward seeing someone as an adult at 18 years old instead of 21 years old. With the power of voting being brought closer to her at a young age, she sought to yield it. She proposed that students' rights and voices must be respected by the powers that be, especially the Iowa State Board of Regents' policies. Wagner then outlined the range of power afforded to students, from economic to legal, including the "power to litigate to obtain redress."

She concluded, "Students also have the power to call into public question the efficacy and ability of those whose purpose to govern in the public interest. In other words, we have power."


IT WAS A crisp fall day on September 27, 1975, and a strong wind was whipping through the nearly 500 Iowa State University students gathered on the steps of Curtiss Hall. Their eyes were on the lone speaker in front of them. Behind the podium stood Cornelius Henry, chairman of the Black Student Organization. Dressed in dark sunglasses and an open black jean jacket revealing a white shirt underneath, he shouted above the wind. A banner with the words DOES JUSTICE MEAN JUST US? rippled behind him. To his right, the words JACK TRICE STADIUM were painted on a sign.

His speech followed Jane Larkin, an Iowa State graduate who spoke about the historical significance of racial injustices at the state and national levels. She spoke of profit and the power of division to sow racism. A guerilla theater group had also reenacted the case from the previous summer of Edward Larmond, a Black Iowa State University student who was sentenced to 10 years for forgery while the White female also involved in the case was set free without punishment. During the sentencing scene, the man playing Larmond stood up and yelled, "This is a mockery of justice! A mockery. A mockery!" The words echoed off the nearby campus buildings.

Henry began by calling out the athletic department and the fact that despite having 40 percent Black football players, only one assistant coach was Black. The lack of Black representation on the faculty was also highlighted. A list of demands was circulated among the audience. Murmurs of approval rose up as the audience began reading them. Several waved the papers above their heads.

Henry pointed out that there had been a recent change in the White House. Now, he said, referring to the color of the Iowa State University administration building, perhaps it was time for a change in the Grey House. He left the podium and asked who was going to march to the Grey House with him. He gathered 60 students behind him and marched to President Pearson's office, demands in hand. Many of the demands were the same as those relayed to Pearson on May 17, 1974, in Parks's office. But farther down the list, there was something new: There was a demand that the new football stadium be named for Jack Trice.

# 12

# The First
# Regents Meeting

THE NEXT YEAR, IN 1976, JILL WAGNER LOOKED AROUND THE TABLE OF
the conference room of Fisher-Nickell House. It was the original home
economics building designed to teach women the art of cooking and
baby care. It was also the same room where she had lobbied Parks for
women's health rights just a few months earlier.

She had also recently played a pivotal role in making the football
stadium experience "safer." The football crowds had gotten so rowdy
that certain areas had to become designated hard-hat areas due to
flying projectiles being launched toward the field. Student-section
rowdiness was the rule, not the exception. Several opening coin tosses
and kickoffs had to be delayed because the students swarmed the field
before the game even began. Wagner had been part of the team working
with the athletic council that negotiated a new set of guidelines for
student conduct at games. One of the more memorable rule additions
included banning fruit from the stadium lest it be used as a weapon.
Beer was also banned from the stands, as the bottles often found their

way onto the field. Now, as president of the GSB, Jill was championing an even bigger decision regarding the new football stadium. This was to be an official meeting of the Advisory Committee on the Naming of Buildings and Streets.

Following her inauguration address, Jill had made good on her promise to empower the students of Iowa State University. The GSB was now the "employer" of the Iowa State faculty. The Public Employment Relations Board (PER) ruled that Iowa State employees were not employed by the university or the Iowa Board of Regents. Instead, according to a 1976 spokesman for the PER, "Iowa State students are the only persons in a position to make judgments about their instructors, and the GSB is the chosen representative body of the students."

The GSB had also polled 3,000 students on the stadium issue, and more than 70 percent indicated their preference for the name Jack Trice Stadium. The student movement was described by one letter writer as a "sincere, broad-based, reasonable request to name the stadium after a student-athlete whose short life and death symbolize many things dear to the institution and standards it espouses."

Gary Mulhall, a member of the Iowa State University Foundation—a group largely concerned with university fundraising—had sponsored an opposing petition calling for the name Cyclone Stadium. Because of how the money was handled at the time, the ISU Foundation actually owned the stadium and rented it to Iowa State University for one dollar a year. When the debts on the stadium were paid, the foundation would then gift the stadium to the university.

"I feel that many people have an interest in naming the stadium other than just those on campus," Mulhall told the *Daily* in 1976. Mulhall's petition was not sent directly to the students, but they were encouraged to sign it if they agreed that the name Cyclone Stadium would "honor all Cyclone players of the past, including Jack Trice, and the future." Mulhall was also quick to point out that despite the foundation being a fundraising organization, the decision to name the stadium ultimately fell on others. In this case, the regents had the final say and would likely take their cue from Parks's Advisory Committee on the Naming of Buildings and Streets. Mulhall's efforts were bolstered when a brochure offering advance tickets for the 1976 football season referred to the "New Cyclone Stadium." That didn't sit well with Wagner and many of her GSB colleagues, who felt it was a clear effort by the athletic department to influence the naming committee.

Charles Sohn had also heard of the naming committee meeting and the list of possible names being proposed. As he was not a member of any of the naming committees, he let his opinion be known in print. In a letter to the *Daily* editors, he scoffed at the idea that someone would suggest Parks Stadium, one of the options. Another proposition, Alumni Stadium, would be an honor to all who had attended ISU, himself included. But Sohn jabbed that it would "also honor the son of a bitch across the hall in my dorm who was here less than a year and stole my stamp collection on his way out."

As to the unwritten motivation to honor those who had donated to the school, Sohn sarcastically wrote, "Trice didn't give a cent to this place." One couldn't be considered "a major donor just by coming to Iowa State to study agriculture to help southern Black farmers (like that Carver guy) or just by integrating an athletic program for the love of sport."

In fact, Sohn remarked tongue-in-cheek, "Blacks who thought they deserved playing for a major school in the 1920s didn't show good sense, especially those who got killed doing it."

Instead Cyclone Stadium would honor all athletes. Even Sohn's friend Dan who once "beat up three students in a downtown bar without breaking a sweat. He's in a penitentiary now, but he'll get all nostalgic when he hears of 'Cyclone Stadium.'"

Sohn, again sarcastically, concluded in his letter how clever and distinctive the name would be. It would look "nice" in the phone book among Cyclone Inn, Cyclone Motors, Cyclone Restaurant, and Cyclone Trophy Company. In this vein, the student senate seemingly voted to include "Cyclone" in the names of all the buildings on campus. Why should any one person be singled out for an honor?

Wagner was only one of three students on the naming committee that day. It was actually the second meeting to name the stadium, as the first meeting had been postponed because of poor faculty member attendance. This time, however, Wagner would have her say. She would speak for the will of the students.

The conference room was filled with faculty and alumni. It was a combination of an ad-hoc advisory committee President Parks had put together as well as the official naming committee. This would be the day they would come up with the official recommendation that Parks would present to the regents. It would then be at the regents meeting in a few days where the name they chose would be officially voted on and adopted.

After a preliminary discussion, the list of six proposed names was quickly whittled down to just two contenders: Jack Trice Stadium and Cyclone Stadium. There were no surprises there. The conversation quickly turned to public sentiment on the stadium naming.

Student vice president Don Morris, who joined Wagner on the committee, spoke up and summed up the situation: "The students support Trice stadium. Alums support Cyclone Stadium. And the faculty and staff are split."

No one disputed him.

The naming committee chairman, Virgil Lagomarcino, who knew the students well as the first dean of the College of Education, remarked that several petitions supporting Jack Trice Stadium had indeed come across his desk over the last two years. Wagner reiterated that thousands of students had signed those petitions.

Lagomarcino responded that, on the other hand, he had received significant communication from alumni and friends of the university who overwhelmingly supported the name Cyclone Stadium. Three of the other faculty members on the naming committee agreed. Virtually every letter they had received in the mail supported Cyclone Stadium. They also agreed that the Iowa State students weren't exactly the "letter-writing type." The letters, they clarified, didn't seek to "degrade Jack Trice, but to make the stadium name more encompassing to include other deserving athletes."

To this, Morris wondered out loud, for all to hear, what then to make of Jack Trice's exceptional character. Had he not paid the "highest price" for his school?

"Anyone who goes out for any Cyclone team makes a sacrifice," replied one of the engineering faculty. "It's a matter of degrees." He added that a generic name such as Cyclone Stadium could be more easily identified with Iowa State University athletics.

Another faculty member argued that students had short memories and future generations likely would forget what the name Jack Trice meant or even who he was.

Wagner quickly retorted, "I question how many students know how the term 'Cyclone' came to be associated with Iowa State teams." The nickname had come from an 1895 *Chicago Tribune* article declaring, "Northwestern might as well have tried to play football with an Iowa Cyclone." From there, the name stuck.

Finally the conversation came to an end. No further deliberation was taken up. The 14 committee members in the room each voted in turn. Parks tallied up the numbers. The three students in the room had voted for Jack Trice Stadium. The remaining 11 members had voted for Cyclone Stadium. Cyclone Stadium would be recommended to the regents.

THE DAY OF the regents meeting arrived. On May 14, 1976, Wagner and several of her fellow student government members packed into her friend's old station wagon. They were determined not to give up on Jack Trice. Munching on snacks, they drove the nearly three hours on I-80 to Council Bluffs and pulled into the parking lot for the Iowa School for the Deaf. They found their way to the room where the regents meeting would take place and took their seats. Officially everyone had a right to be heard at these meetings, and she and Don Morris would speak for the students.

That morning, the *Daily* published the results of its own faculty telephone survey. It had contacted the members of the Faculty Council. Of the 27 members who were not at the meeting with Parks, 23 had said their opinion was never even solicited on the issue. Of the remaining four who did speak to the council representative, three said they favored Jack Trice's name.

Prior to the meeting, there had been talk that the field itself might be named for Jack but not the actual stadium. A letter that same day to the *Daily* criticized this notion as equating Jack with a doormat. To name the Astroturf for him would be to symbolically walk all over him, it argued. In that vein, the writer proposed a senior gift of a bench named after President Parks. It would provide the students a proper place to put their rears.

Parks began the discussion at the regents meeting by recounting the history of the stadium, its planning, and its reconstruction. He then clarified that the university did not yet own the stadium. It was still owned by the ISU Foundation. Finally, he reiterated the formation of the ad-hoc naming committee and the recommendation by the official university naming committee that the new stadium be named Cyclone Stadium.

Wagner and Morris were recognized and given their turn on the floor. A petition signed by more than 1,300 students was presented to the regents. Morris began by reading Jack's letter out loud. He recounted Jack's words and how he knew the honor of his race and his family were at stake before he took those unknowingly fateful steps onto the football field. He knew when he put on the Iowa State uniform that day that he was expected to do great things. When he finished reading, Morris looked up and down the line of regents' faces.

"What he stood for and what he believed can inspire all Iowa State athletes," Morris concluded. "That statement means more than the name Cyclone. This would be an inspiration."

Wagner followed Don's statement by asking those in attendance about heroism. Something, she said, was weighing on the conscience of the nation, and it needed to find itself again. "Heroes," Wagner said. "We need heroes." She described how following Vietnam, her generation needed someone to look up to. The students of Iowa State University were thirsty for someone and something to believe in. In an age conspicuously without heroes, she wondered, why was the memory of Jack Trice so objectionable? "Trice is hero material for the student body," Wagner continued.

She then went on to recount the many buildings on campus named for contributors to the university. Was Jack not the ultimate contributor? Was someone else wronged or excluded when the science building was named or the administration hall dedicated? "[Jack] represented worthwhile values and was a dear and high contributor to the essence of Iowa State," Wagner said. She concluded, "Jack is someone we would like to look up to."

The lone student on the board of regents, Steven Zumbach, also spoke up. He agreed with Wagner and said, "You can't be on that campus and not feel the support for Jack Trice."

Wagner and Morris returned to their seats and looked to the board members. One of the board members made a motion to adopt Parks's recommendation of Cyclone Stadium. But before the vote could commence, Zumbach proposed an alternative. As a student, he didn't want to see the fight lost on that day. He asked out loud how the university could name something they didn't own.

Another regent, Ray Bailey, agreed he was on to something and said, "I can't see us naming a building we don't own."

The regents debated among themselves. The recommendation by Parks and the naming committee would be accepted. That seemed a given. The process for selecting the name was not flawed and should be honored. But the question of whether the regents and not the ISU Foundation could name the stadium was still left unanswered.

Something that many people later felt was unsaid that evening was that the regents hoped that by delaying the formal vote, the students in front of them would graduate and hopefully take the issue with them into the sunset. Zumbach, as the students' inside man, was buying the students time, but the motion may also have given the opposition an out as well. It wasn't clear who would win by the delay tactic, but most people thought Jack's support was fleeting.

Still, regent Harry Slife expressed concern with the new motion. He said they were probably just delaying the inevitable and asked what good that would do for an already divided university. "I don't think any kind of unanimity will emerge," he said. "We just may make it worse by delaying a decision."

Nevertheless, the motion to delay naming the stadium up to four years (a notable number of years, indeed) was made and passed 6–2. Parks spoke up and asked the board to clarify what it meant by "deferral." He said the timing of everything concerned him very much. He asked the board to also explain more clearly why it had recommended deferral. Clearly he wasn't happy with the decision.

Board president Mary Louise Petersen noted that no one was critical of the procedure involved for Iowa State University to name the stadium. But as they had said earlier, two things still stood out: 1) the building did not yet belong to the university and 2) the intensity of the student feeling to name the building Jack Trice Stadium was significant, whereas there did not appear to be that same feeling of intensity for Cyclone Stadium.

Immediately Morris spoke up and asked how the stadium would be referred to until the actual naming occurred. "That will be crucial," he said.

Parks responded to him that all university publications would call it Iowa State Stadium or simply "the football stadium." Of course there may be some slip-ups here and there, he said, where someone called it Cyclone Stadium. After all, practically everything on campus already bore the Cyclone name.

The meeting concluded. Morris stood up and began expressing his frustration to the student reporter standing off to the side. "The administration has always requested that students work within existing channels," he said. "In the case of Jack Trice, students researched his history, educated others, and overwhelmingly supported the naming of the stadium after Jack. We as members of the students' representative body, the GSB, went on record in favor of naming the stadium after

Jack. Ignoring the students' representation is the equivalent of having no representation at all."

Wagner, meanwhile, sat there silently. At first she was shocked by the board's action. Without saying a word, she got up and walked over to the snack area in the corner of the room. As she got up, a reporter from the *Des Moines Register* who was in the audience approached her. The reporter asked her what she thought of the regents' decision.

Wagner reached down and picked up a piece of yellow sponge cake. She examined it and put in her mouth. A sudden sense of satisfaction came across her face. "You know, I thought we had one chance in a million of overturning an official university committee recommendation," she said, munching on the piece of cake. "I really didn't expect this, but I'm actually happy with the delay."

Then, turning to walk away, she added, "Time will tell if student sentiment in Jack Trice is just an ideal."

# 13
# The Great Compromise

"ANYTIME THE STUDENTS AND UNIVERSITY OFFICIALS HAVE A FIGHT, AND it winds up in a tie, the students have the right to celebrate as if they won an overwhelming victory."

That's how *Des Moines Register* columnist Don Kaul described the regents' decision to postpone the stadium naming. The skids had been greased in the university's favor, he wrote, but the students and the Jack Trice movement lived on to fight another day. He pointed out, of course, that delaying the vote up to four years should be sufficient for the student agitators to move on with their lives and leave the good fight behind.

Kaul was an irreverent two-time Pulitzer Prize finalist with a tight moral compass. His columns provided a broad range of commentary on everything from girls' high school basketball games to gun rights, always sharpened by a dry, scathing wit. He eschewed electric typewriters for manual ones and rode his bike everywhere. In fact, he helped cofound the RAGBRAI (the Register's Annual Great Bicycle Ride Across Iowa), which started out as a column assignment and grew to become a seven-day roving festival well known in the biking world.

It is believed to be the oldest, largest, and longest multiday bicycle touring event.

Kaul's signature look was a pair of dark sunglasses, a mustache, and hair flopping just below his ears. The first day he walked into the *Des Moines Register* newsroom, he found it "a beat-up scruffy place filled with beat-up scruffy people, almost all men. They worked in a big room lined with gray steel desks piled high with newspapers, stacks of books, notebooks, and ashtrays overflowing with cigarette stubs." The men wrote on big black typewriters next to big black rotary phones. It was a case of love at first sight. "This is my kind of place," Kaul had told himself.

Kaul had a strong sense of social justice, and when something rubbed him the wrong way, when there were kinks in the bike chains of society, he called them out. In the days after Martin Luther King Jr.'s assassination, Kaul wrote, "They say that a lone assassin pulled the trigger.... They say that every society has its demented individuals and that a society cannot be held responsible for their acts.... It would be comforting to believe that were so—but it is not."

Kaul believed that if the assassin was indeed a sick man, it was "because we are a sick society; sick with hatred, sick with racism, Black and white." In that same column, he recounted two high school boys contacting him just a few hours after Dr. King succumbed to his injuries. They were shaken not only by the civil rights leader's death but also by what they had just witnessed.

The two boys had been in a bowling alley earlier in the evening. It was ladies' night, and the lanes were crowded with women. The news that Dr. King had been shot earlier was already common knowledge, and many of the women present had been discussing it in between their turns. The sound of pins falling mixed with the harmonizing of the Everly Brothers and the belting vocals of Aretha Franklin. Then the music stopped and word came over the loudspeakers that Dr. King had died. It was at that very moment, as the owner finished his tragic announcement, that 10 to 15 women burst into applause.

"There they were," wrote Kaul. "These women—housewives, mothers, members of clubs—and their immediate reaction to the death of a great man was one of glee. That's our society."

It was for reasons such as this that from his desk at the paper Kaul began to take notice of the Jack Trice student movement and what it stood for. He called Jack "the stuff of which legends are made."

In one of his "Over the Coffee" columns, Kaul mused:

All right-thinking persons want to name that stadium after Jack Trice, but society opposes them. (By society, I mean the people who name stadia.) The right-thinkers have attacked the problem in the traditional way, society's way. They have attempted to convince the people who name stadia of the rightness of their cause. They have written letters, they have circulated petitions, they have held meetings. They have failed. When approached on the subject of Trice, the people who name stadia mumble. They mumble low, they mumble high, and soon the question is borne aloft on clouds of mumble. (One suspects that society would prefer to name the stadium after Nelson Rockefeller or some equally worthy pigeon, assuming a suitable donation, but perhaps that's a misreading of the mumbles.)

As the original Jack Trice Memorial Stadium Committee members graduated, Charles Sohn and Alan Beals continued what they termed "on-campus agitation." Sohn appreciated Kaul's support on a larger stage but also felt he was a bit flippant. In one of his columns, Kaul imagined a phone call with Notre Dame's Knute Rockne. Rockne had died in 1931, so naturally it was a long-distance phone call from Iowa. (Fortunately, Kaul had the charges reversed.)

Kaul asked Rockne what he thought of naming the stadium after Jack Trice. Rockne responded by saying he loved the idea. In fact, he once had a full PR team working on creating Notre Dame's own legend, and all they were left with was the Gipper. George Gipp was a drunk, a womanizer, and a gambler whom Rockne recruited out of a pool hall. Imagine, he told Kaul, what he could have done with the material Jack Trice was made from.

It was Kaul's columns about Jack that first caught the attention of many of the incoming Iowa State University students. The early 1980s were a time of political change on campus and across the country. The White House was transitioning from the Democratic Carter administration to the Republican Reagan administration. It was called the Reagan Revolution. Similarly, on campus a more "conservative" ideology had emerged.

But despite the changing political climate, there were still many students in the Iowa State community who had been raised in the shadow of student activism. A new generation of the Jack Trice Memorial Stadium Committee was being formed. Each year, old members would graduate and new students would join the fight. The baton, or rather the football, was continually handed off. It was a linked chain going back years, even decades. In the previous generation of the Jack Trice Memorial Stadium Committee, the students of the 1970s took their fight to the university administration. This time, the 1980s iteration would take their argument straight to the people.

Many of the new Iowa State University students had been born in the early 1960s. They were old enough to remember hearing and seeing the civil rights movement and turmoil of the late 1960s and early '70s on their boxy television sets. Even though many were in elementary school at the time, they could still remember the headlines of the assassination deaths of Martin Luther King Jr. and Robert Kennedy in 1968. Some even remembered *NBC Nightly News* covering the Kent State massacre on the day it occurred, May 4, 1970.

Terry Rickers was one of those new student activists. He had grown up on a farm in western Iowa. He helped his family raise hogs. In the fall he would catch Iowa State football games on the radio and dream about attending the school when he was older. He was quite intelligent, but he found that differential equations didn't agree with him. So he switched his major from nuclear engineering to pursue law like his favorite TV hero, Perry Mason.

When Kaul shared the details of Jack Trice's tragic injury and subsequent death while wearing the colors of Iowa State in his columns, Rickers was both shocked and fascinated. Jack's commitment to represent Iowa State University and play football despite racial prejudice convinced Rickers he was both a trailblazer and a hero.

Rickers entered Iowa State as a freshman in 1978, two years after the regents meeting to delay the stadium naming. As programming director and a DJ for the student radio station, he mixed with a more diverse crowd than most students, including members of the Black Student Organization (BSO).

Rick Yoder was Rickers' friend and also a co–GSB senator. Like Rickers, Yoder first became aware of Jack's story through Don Kaul's columns. Compared to the tumultuous 1960s and '70s, Yoder felt that campus on the cusp and into the 1980s had probably grown quieter and on average more politically conservative. But he still felt there was a wide enough opening in the divisive politics that he could help drive a wedge along the cracked line.

Yoder had run for GSB using a picture of then–secretary of state Alexander Haig saying, "I'm in control." At the time, it was a common parody to reference Haig's erroneous claim he was in control of the government when Reagan was shot in March 1981. Yoder ran on a progressive platform and often called out President Parks and much of his administration. Yoder's campaign rallies often used a refrain from the 1979 Talking Heads song "Life During Wartime": "This ain't no party. This ain't no disco. This ain't no fooling around."

When not campaigning or governing, Yoder spent much of his free time working as an assistant manager for the on-campus watering hole the Maintenance Shop. The M-Shop, as it was called, was a small brick-and-stained-glass venue that doubled as a nightclub and gathering spot for social activists on campus. For decades the vibration from the music coming through the M-Shop's speakers could be felt rumbling throughout the Memorial Union, shaking the leaky ceiling overhead. The M-Shop's ceiling was a remnant from its original days as an actual maintenance department in the school's basement. Fridays were especially popular when Yoder and his fellow GSB senators served patrons, and themselves, anywhere from 60 to 90 kegs of beer.

The manager of the Maintenance Shop was Dan Rice, an Ames college student who had taken a hiatus from classes to run the venue. His grandfather was an Iowa State yearbook editor the year Jack died. Rebellion was in his blood, for that same grandfather was later expelled for "extreme student activism." Rice had already founded and conducted an open noontime forum on social justice issues at the M-Shop called "We've Gotta Talk…." One of the most popular topics always seemed to be the Jack Trice movement. Interest sometimes ebbed and flowed depending on current GSB leadership, but Jack's spirit was always there, even if it was just sitting on a stool sipping a beer in the background.

When Yoder became a GSB senator, he made a concerted effort to promote the Jack Trice Memorial Stadium Committee and encouraged

Rice to keep the movement regularly in the spotlight. Tom Emmerson, the Iowa State University journalism professor who had written the original article on Jack, would sometimes join these "We've Gotta Talk…" forums to discuss Jack's history and sacrifice. His appearance at the forums—in addition to frequently dropping in on the editors of the *Iowa State Daily* to nonchalantly encourage them to cover Jack, as he described it—became a "guerilla operation." He would water the seeds whenever he could.

Meanwhile, while the progressive students were discussing social issues and Jack Trice over beer at the M-Shop, another student was discussing Jack's story with the Black athletes of the Black Student Organization. As a Black man on campus, Ed Freeman often found himself surrounded by members of the BSO and, by association, many of the Iowa State athletes. There were still only a few hundred Black students on campus, and a large percentage of that group was composed of male athletes, so an organic connection grew between the athletic community and the BSO.

Although he was not an athlete himself, Freeman felt a kinship with Jack Trice. As African Americans, they both looked up to George Washington Carver as a model of success. Freeman had taken it upon himself to seek out the letters between Carver and Iowa State University to better understand the man and what he accomplished at the school. Freeman had also come across Jack's letter, and found it spoke to him as well. The more Freeman learned about Jack, the more he could relate to him. Jack had majored in animal husbandry like Carver before him. Freeman had entered those same halls of science in pursuit of medical school.

Most of the time, on campus and around Ames, Freeman found himself in an inviting atmosphere. Like Jack, he had chosen Iowa State for its academic rigors knowing Black students were still a minority.

Still, he hadn't found any major racial roadblocks. It was clear to him and the other students he was a minority, but he found the differences manageable. Yet Freeman, like many of the BSO students, believed the minority students on campus deserved something more. Jack Trice deserved something more. As fellow Black students, they felt the stadium should be named for Jack.

They often pointed to the nearby University of Iowa as an example of why Iowa State should honor Jack. In 1972, inspired by another sportswriter's columns, the University of Iowa had named its football stadium for alumnus Nile Kinnick. The school had cited Kinnick's winning of the Heisman Trophy and subsequent death during a WWII navy training flight in 1943 as proof of his accomplishment and sacrifice. Kinnick had also been inducted into the College Football Hall of Fame in 1951. Kinnick had won out over a smaller attempt to honor the University of Iowa's own African American football pioneer Duke Slater. (Notably, the University of Iowa regents would go on to support the field at Kinnick Stadium being named for Slater in 2021.)

Freeman believed in the righteousness of the Jack Trice movement, but he didn't want it to be seen as a "Black-only" thing. So many righteous movements could be ignored or dismissed by labeling them the actions of "angry Black men." So when the opportunity arose to cochair the Jack Trice Memorial Stadium Committee along with GSB senator Rick Yoder, Freeman jumped at it.

Yoder and Freeman made a sort of odd couple as cochairs of the Jack Trice Memorial Stadium Committee. Yoder was a White progressive activist who loved listening to punk music. Freeman was a serious Black student focusing on his premedical studies. But when it came to honoring Jack Trice, their visions aligned. One of their largest efforts to raise money was an auction in 1982. Yoder, Freeman, and several of their friends organized the event and solicited items to be donated.

Cookbooks, artwork, cartoons, and autographed memorabilia all hit the auction block. They also invited Don Kaul to be their guest speaker.

In his keynote speech, Kaul said college athletes of the day were being treated like big-business professionals. That type of focus stood in contrast to earlier times when college sports embodied the spirit of amateurism. That spirit once existed and should exist again, he said. Jack Trice represented that spirit. Even if Jack's skin color wasn't considered, or the fact that he died playing football, his belief in and love for the game and pursuit of excellence in student athletics should be honored. College sports shouldn't be about school paydays; they should be about the idealism of athletics that Jack embodied.

During his own speech, Anthony Williams—who later became the GSB's first Black president—stood up and said he was fed up with the administration's opposition to naming the stadium for Jack. They shouldn't have to raise money for Jack. He should be honored like all the other athletes who didn't have the money to back their accomplishments. He shouldn't need to buy his memorial. Others agreed and said the memory of Jack needed to be kept alive or it would die out.

The evening festivities concluded with a bluegrass band and the formal auction. A football signed by the Iowa State University team brought in $45, which was significant compared to the least valued item of the night—$9 for an autographed picture of President Reagan. In a column following the fundraiser, Kaul addressed some misgivings people may have had about his brand of sarcasm. He made it clear that the Jack Trice movement was no joke. It meant a lot to him and to the other people involved. He reiterated the story for his readers. He said he described Jack's letter as "corny" because any form of idealism connected to sports must seem to many people as just a corny idea. But it was the innocence in Jack's letter that touched him. It reminded

Kaul of a time when athletes went out for a team, before they were recruited by fawning coaches promising them the world. Naming the stadium for Jack would be a nod to the core values of college athletics rather than to money and economics. Plus, if they didn't name the stadium after Jack, he would never lift the Jack Trice curse.

What was this curse? It was of Kaul's making. Months earlier Kaul had begun to invoke a Jack Trice curse whenever the Iowa State football team failed to perform. It was a tongue-in-cheek gesture meant to keep the fight alive. The curse wasn't the ghost of Jack Trice, of course; it was an example of Kaul's patented absurdism meant to keep a topic in the limelight. He described it as an unassuming creature built from spare bicycle parts masquerading as a tailgate party. If you saw the curse on the street, you might mistake it for an old 1950s Chevrolet. Logically, in the instances when Iowa State did win, Kaul admitted he must have forgotten to bring the curse with him.

For the next year after the 1982 fundraiser, the student effort continued en masse. The GSB, including Yoder and Rickers, raised money to fund a billboard on Lincoln Way, Ames's busiest street. The sign declared to all who entered, WELCOME TO AMES—HOME OF JACK TRICE MEMORIAL STADIUM. While Sohn wasn't directly involved in the billboard project, he told the *Des Moines Register* at the time, "It will probably annoy some administrators. And I think that's just fine." The students also hired a pilot to fly a banner over the crowds at football games. Flying among the clouds were the words, WELCOME TO JACK TRICE STADIUM. Another small victory came one weekend when the TV commentators mistakenly announced the game was being broadcast live from Jack Trice Stadium.

Like all college football games, tailgates at Iowa State University were an integral tradition, but in the 1980s, they often became rallying events for the Jack Trice movement. Jack Trice tailgates became regular occurrences. Cars were spray-painted with slogans of support for Trice. Bumper stickers were slapped onto whatever they could stick to. Students in the stands wore black armbands and the school band wore white armbands on the field in Jack's memory. Groups across a diverse spectrum, from the Home Economics Advisory Council to the Council on Fraternities, organized events and donated money to the cause.

But despite what seemed like progress and forward momentum, each step of the way, the administration would lay down roadblocks. "Beware of mass interference!" Jack had said. For many in positions of bureaucratic importance, it was too hot of an issue to take on directly. Several students and faculty members approached Parks asking to dedicate a game to Jack at halftime. Parks informed the committee that the athletic department deemed the tribute "too political." They had never dedicated a halftime to a cause before, and they weren't going to start with Jack. To the students on the committee, however, the pushback from the athletic department seemed to be based on something other than honoring Jack's memory. It did seem political, but for an entirely different reason.

At the time, the athletic department and some members of the Jack Trice Memorial Stadium Committee had recently butted heads over a controversial incident. An Iowa State University football player had been caught setting up a prank and beat up the student who caught him. The athlete later pled guilty to simple assault. That the football player was still allowed to remain on the team caused somewhat of a stir on campus.

Fearing that athletes were receiving preferential treatment, the GSB passed a resolution that declared participating in intercollegiate athletics was a privilege and, as representatives of the university, athletes should be responsible for their behavior off the field. If an athlete was convicted of violent criminal behavior, he should be barred from competition.

Several members of the GSB who orchestrated the resolution, including Yoder, happened to also be members of the Jack Trice Memorial Stadium Committee. This did not go unnoticed by the athletic department and clearly shaded its view of the committee members and the department's willingness to cooperate with them.

The alumni also continued their years-long aversion to naming the stadium after Jack, some for admittedly more revolting reasons than others. In one particularly shameful incident, during a game when the students were wearing black armbands for Jack, Tamra Ortgies-Young and her friend Teresa, who was Black, were passing out leaflets in support of renaming the stadium after Jack. Ortgies-Young was the director of communications for the GSB and spearheaded many of the public relations aspects of the campaign. She helped record several radio spots with the Iowa State University football players supporting the campaign and ran them on the Cyclone radio network.

"I have never seen the campus as united as it was on that day," Ortgies-Young recalled in a letter to the *Ames Tribune* editor published in 1987. "But still we felt confident until we came to an alumnus with several diamond rings and a Bloody Mary in her hand who said right in front of Teresa, 'Jack Trice? I don't want our new stadium named after some [N-word].'"

Although Teresa tried to focus on the positive experiences that day, she still was shocked to see something in real life she had only read about—blatant, overt racism. It smacked her sharply in the face. The racist woman threw the flyer on the wet ground and walked away. Ortgies-Young, still shaking, picked up the crumpled flyer. She looked down at it, but all she could see in her hands was the face of a woman from historical newsreels screaming about the need for segregation.

AS 1983 WOUND down, the final payments on the stadium were being made, which meant the time to officially name the stadium had finally arrived. The wheels had been set in motion a year earlier. The regents would vote on the stadium name at their next meeting. Several students and faculty members on the Jack Trice Memorial Stadium Committee planned their strategy—who would speak and what they would say. Some would focus on inclusiveness, others on racism. But they would all highlight how important Jack's story was and that for nearly a decade they had kept up the fight. Students had come and gone, but Jack was always there.

Just days before the meeting, Parks announced that the stadium, which many referred to as No-Name Stadium, would be named Cyclone Stadium as planned. But he would insist that the field inside be called Jack Trice Field. This way he would ensure both names would be represented in some capacity. Many students and the media labeled the idea as a Solomon-like proposal, referencing the biblical tale told in 1 Kings 3:16–28. In it two women both claimed to be the mother of the same infant boy. Solomon offered to split the child in half, knowing that the true mother would relinquish any claims of custody, as she would rather her child live with another as his mother than be killed.

"I'd determined to bring this to a close," Parks told the *Des Moines Register* in December 1983. "It had opened wounds that will be hard to heal." He recognized that while the co-naming wouldn't please everyone, it was a "reasonable accommodation" and dubbed it a "harmonious combination of names."

Sohn, though, questioned the timing of Parks' announcement. He wondered if Parks and the administration hadn't made their intentions known ahead of time because a large-scale poll demonstrating widespread support for Jack Trice Stadium would be published soon.

Some members of the committee, however, saw the compromise as a way of gaining some ground in the fight. Even if it wasn't an absolute victory, it did take some land from the enemy and kept Jack's name—and perhaps the movement—alive.

Mike Keller was an *Iowa State Daily* editor and the GSB vice president at the time. He was a member of the Jack Trice Memorial Stadium Committee and friends with Dan Rice and Rick Yoder. When he got wind of the compromise, he was of the opinion that they should jump on it. Not because it was the end result they wanted but because it was a stepping-stone to something better. If the field was named for Jack, it might be just a matter of time before the stadium name itself was changed. He didn't think the clunky phrase Jack Trice Field at Cyclone Stadium was sustainable. Jack could hopefully win that war of jumbled words. Plus, as an editor, he was confident the student press would refer to it just as Jack Trice Field anyway and drop the Cyclone Stadium part. A compromise was a way to get past some of the resistance put up by the wall of alumni money. Some members of the Jack Trice Memorial Stadium Committee would go to the meeting looking for a Hail Mary, but others might just settle for a field goal and points on the board.

IT WAS A frigid Thursday evening when the regents finally met on December 15, 1983, at the University of Northern Iowa in Cedar Falls. Weather had kept one regent from attending at all. Parks began the meeting by acknowledging the strong student sentiment for naming the stadium after Jack Trice but reminded the regents that Cyclone Stadium was the official name chosen by the university. Recognizing a need to appease the opposition, he took the initiative to craft a compromise of both names that would still honor Jack. He assured those in attendance that all Cyclones players who knew the Jack Trice story would be pleased to be associated with Jack. "And from what we know about Jack Trice," Parks said, "he'd be pleased to have his name identified with 'Cyclone.' He was a Cyclone and was proud of that." Further, Parks was bound to the 1976 recommendation. "I would lack credibility if I didn't remain committed to that," he said.

Sohn, who had accompanied the students to the meeting, asked for a delay of his own. It was finals week, and the next regents meeting was scheduled to take place on the Iowa State University campus. Further, many of the students didn't even find out about the scheduled vote until the last minute. Parks disagreed with Sohn. He felt they had waited long enough, and he believed the compromise was "congenial and homogeneous." Sohn fought back. He turned and pleaded with the regents. "Don't make Jack Trice a second-class citizen," he said.

Sohn said he was speaking that day for 10 years of work by thousands of people who supported the name Jack Trice Stadium. He explained to the board why people felt so strongly about naming the stadium for Jack Trice. He spoke of Jack's ancestors who had been slaves and then struggled to become independent after emancipation. He spoke of how Jack valued education. Sohn's plea resonated with at least two of the regents sitting on the dais, for they also understood what it was like to be considered less than others. They knew what it was like to fight against the status quo of oppression.

One was Peggy Anderson, a self-described feminist. Though not the only female on the regents board, she was often seen as a voice for women's interests. She had come to the board as a local pioneer for women's rights in the 1970s. She was the first woman to sit on the Cedar Falls School Board, a position she purposely pursued after being told by the mayor, "We wouldn't feel comfortable with a woman on the council."

Anderson had not attended any of the Iowa schools. Instead she had gone to Smith University. From that standpoint, she considered herself an outsider. The other people on the board had far closer associations with the Iowa universities and alumni networks. As a result, she often found herself voting in the minority, but she saw herself and her vote as representing the interests of both students and disenfranchised groups.

Even though she considered many of the other regents to be "thoughtful and nice people," to her they always represented a "good old boys'" club that was "pretty willing to listen to what the administration wanted them to do." She respected Iowa State University and Parks but believed they lacked foresight.

Anderson often stood on the same side of issues as another regent, Percy Harris. Harris was Cedar Rapids's first Black physician and would go on to become a bedrock member of the community. He was born in Mississippi just before the Great Depression and had lost both his parents and a sister by the time he was 12 years old. After his mother's death, he spent two years in a tuberculosis sanatorium. Harris became medical staff president at St. Luke's Hospital in Cedar Rapids in 1976 and the following year was appointed as the first Black member of the Iowa Board of Regents.

The remainder of the board was composed of the state chairman of the Republican Party, a former lieutenant governor, a longtime alumnus of Iowa, the wife of a wealthy university supporter who had passed away, and the wife of a prominent hog farmer. That left one newly appointed member—Timothy Neville, who had only been on the board a few weeks.

Adverse weather had begun approaching, so many of the building's occupants were eager to leave. But one vote still lay before them. Harris spoke up: "I don't' know when it became fashionable for Blacks to participate in athletics, but at ISU that barrier was broken 60 years ago." He continued, "It so happened that the person who did it lost his life. It would be unfortunate if we were to lose this opportunity to honor the first Black football player at Iowa State and, probably, one of its first Black students."

Anderson offered her own version of a compromise. Parks had said he took it upon himself to offer the option of separate names for the stadium and field, so she felt she could offer her own. She proposed an equal sharing of the stadium name by calling it Jack Trice–Cyclone Stadium. The University of Iowa had recently named their indoor arena Carver-Hawkeye, signaling a dual name was possible, and Anderson had supported their proposal. Harris signaled his approval for the dual name as well. He said a lot of beauty accompanied the Jack Trice story and the university should not lose this opportunity. Neville, the new regent, also voiced his agreement.

Looking for further support, the three regents found none. The room fell silent, and with it, the dual-naming motion. The remaining five regents voted it down. Anderson and Harris could see the writing on the wall: Jack didn't have the votes.

The inclement weather continued its approach and the people in the room began to stir. The final proposal for Cyclone Stadium and Jack Trice Field was put forth. As dictated by Parks, the outside would be named Cyclone Stadium, but the field inside would be named for Jack. Anderson, Harris, and Neville—realizing they were outnumbered—acquiesced. The proposal passed unanimously.

Just like the first regents meeting, the follow-up question was brought forth as to how the university would use the two names. Parks commented he would ask the university to use both of the names, but he couldn't control what the outside world did. Perhaps unknowingly, Parks left it open to interpretation. The students could do what they

209

pleased. After all, their house was Jack's, and *they* went to Jack Trice Stadium to watch football. Though for some the decision that day felt hollow, others saw it as yet another small victory. They would continue to fight low with their eyes open.

During the next few years, the GSB organized the creation of a Jack Trice statue on campus. The statue was paid for entirely by the students and dedicated after the 1988 VEISHEA parade. The sculptor Chris Bennett was a friend of Dan Rice's from the Maintenance Shop and was honing his craft. The entire process took Bennett approximately a year. The final product stood 6.5 feet tall and weighed more than 1,000 pounds. In the piece, Jack leans on one leg, gazing down at his "last letter." By his foot is a stack of books, one of which has been authored by "C. Sohn." He is dressed not in a football uniform but instead in a collegiate sweater to honor the student side of his story. Jack's grade average was apparently 90 percent. A location for the statue was chosen between the administration building, Beardshear Hall, and Carver Hall.

Don Kaul, who kept up his call to honor Jack in his columns, spoke at the statue dedication ceremony. He continued to lament that the stadium was still named for some windstorm and not for someone who embodied true collegiate athletics. Several of Jack's relatives were also in attendance, including Reverend Chester Trice, who was nine years old when Jack's plaque was first dedicated. His son, Chester Trice Jr., remarked, "This has been a tremendous 15-year relay race. The baton has passed from student to student, from class to class, and without dropping it one time." The statue became a larger and more visible reminder of Jack's presence on campus.

As for Sohn, he was already known by his fellow faculty members for several things: smoking a pipe, occasional grumpiness, and driving an old Singer well past its expiration date. He was not someone who gave things up easily. Once he committed to something, it was almost impossible to sway him. When the *Des Moines Register* asked Sohn what was next, most people already knew the answer: He would continue to fight. He would continue to put his faith in the students. He told the paper, "The story keeps resurfacing. Anytime a young idealist gets a hold of the Jack Trice story, there is tremendous enthusiasm for it." As it turned out, he was right. Jack's spirit wasn't extinguished. He would stay on his toes. He would still do big things.

# 14
## <u>Fists Up!</u>

WHEN MILTON McGRIFF FIRST WALKED ONTO THE CAMPUS OF IOWA STATE University in 1994, he was immediately noticed. It wasn't just that he was a Black graduate student in his mid-50s with a gleaming shaved head. It was that he brought with him decades of resistance grown from a deep understanding of racism in America. He brought with him Black Power.

Milton had grown up in Philadelphia and, like Jack, attended a predominantly White school. He had been adopted as a baby but didn't find out until after his adoptive mother died. In 1963 he joined the National Guard as a radio operator and was stationed near Fort Knox. Once during his service, he was scheduled to fly back home from Louisville to Philadelphia. Unfortunately, he missed his plane and was stuck in town. He was still in uniform, so he went to a downtown bar he knew. It was a place he had frequented numerous times before with other soldiers, both Black and White.

He went up to the bartender and ordered a beer. The young man behind the bar paused and looked McGriff up and down. "I can't serve you," he said.

McGriff immediately became puzzled. He told the bartender he had drank there before. "We sat over there." McGriff motioned to a table in the corner.

"Oh, if you go over there I can serve you, but I can't serve you at the bar," was the bartender's reply. McGriff felt as is if his soul had been laid bare. The uniform he had felt such pride wearing suddenly became worthless. No matter the color of his uniform, it was the color of his skin that dictated where he could have a beer.

As a student he would later tell the *Daily*, "I was standing there in full uniform, for the army, in a town I had not been asked to be sent to, and something died in me in terms of my relationship with the government. I have never really liked the government since."

A realization had come to him. He had been spending his whole life trying to assimilate. He was "being raised to be a white boy." He no longer wanted to step in line.

A year later, at the 1964 Democratic National Convention in Atlantic City, McGriff's passion for activism was sparked again. That was the year the Mississippi Freedom Democratic Party sent their own delegates to the convention. In years past the Mississippi delegates were elected from a traditionally Whites-only Democratic Party, and the same had held true that year. The MFDP had been formed to allow Democrats to elect delegates by both Black and White voters. When the MFDP delegation arrived at the convention dressed in their Sunday best, the White delegates refused to allow the Black delegates to be part of the convention and barred them from voting. McGriff's future wife was working in Atlantic City at the time, and she later told him she saw grown men—Black men—crying on the sidewalk. The democratic system had left them behind. It was then that McGriff declared he "saw the light."

Five years later, McGriff became an early member of the Philadelphia chapter of the Black Panther Party. The Panthers had grown from a revolutionary Black militant group focusing on nationalism, socialism, and self-defense in Oakland, California, in 1966 to a nationwide movement by 1969. As a Black Panther, McGriff felt free for the first time in his life. He spent much of the time delivering Panther literature to neighborhoods, handing out food to children, polling people on the streets, and organizing political activity. He drove himself and other Panthers around the city in a van he commandeered from his salesman job. They also traveled to other states, including New Jersey, where they were arrested in Atlantic City for distributing fliers. McGriff also ran for local political office under the Black Panther Party banner. He felt like he counted for something—like he was doing something right.

From 1969 to 1970, the Black Panther Party and the Philadelphia police were at war. The police raided their headquarters several times and confiscated weapons. The Black Panther headquarters were also firebombed by unknown assailants. Eventually the conflict became too great. Several of the chapter members were forced out of town. Many went back to Oakland. McGriff, however, stayed behind in his hometown. He was a writer and poet at heart. Through the Panthers, his political activism and his pen found a common purpose in Black neighborhood theater. He and other Black writers and actors founded the Black Arts Spectrum Theatre.

One morning in 1969, McGriff was flipping through a copy of *Ramparts*, a magazine promoting progressive politics to middle-class America. He suddenly came across an article that stopped him in his tracks. It was a story of an off-duty police officer in San Francisco who shot and killed a Black man outside his own home. The police officer, Michael O'Brien, was driving back from a sailing trip with his partner.

The two had been drinking. While they were passing through a small, predominantly Black neighborhood, O'Brien lost control of his vehicle. The boat trailer behind his car scraped across a car belonging to Carl Hawkins, a well-known trolley operator in the neighborhood. When he yelled at O'Brien for hitting his car, the off-duty cop got out of his car and drew his service revolver. He pointed it at Hawkins. Hawkins's wife fled into her apartment to call the police, not knowing the two men were officers themselves.

A small crowd quickly grew around O'Brien as he became more and more agitated, waving his gun around in the air. Seething with rage, O'Brien grabbed Hawkins and two other nearby Black residents and forced them up against a wall. Multiple witnesses reported O'Brien yelling, "I want to kill a [N-word]. I want to kill a [N-word] so bad I can taste it."

Hawkins's neighbor, George Baskett, seeing the violent scene unfolding from his porch, quietly removed a wooden slat from his chair and crept behind O'Brien. He swung the slat at O'Brien but missed. O'Brien, in what he claimed was self-defense, turned around and shot Baskett, killing him in broad daylight.

A cry went up from the crowd and the people looking out from their windows. O'Brien fled to a doorway and crouched down. He yelled out, "All you goddamn [N-words], get your heads out the windows. I'll shoot!" In the publicized trial that followed, O'Brien was acquitted of manslaughter charges by an all-White jury. Members of the Black community declared it an example of two justice systems: one for Black people and another for White people.

McGriff found something deep and disturbing about the story. He had to write about it. He sat down at his typewriter and quickly produced a one-act play he called *The Nigger Killer*. He debuted the play in Philadelphia with the help of the Black Arts Spectrum Theatre.

He then moved to New York in 1972 and took the play with him to Lincoln Center as part of a Community/Street Theater Festival. The *New York Times* called it "nonrealistic, but no less disturbing."

The killing took place as a slow-motion ritual. The actors wore masks. The jury was depicted as cardboard posters that looked like shooting gallery targets. The play ended with the actors asking the audience for its verdict. "Guilty," came the answer. Then a chorus of "All power to the people!"

From New York, McGriff made his way to Los Angeles in 1973 as a young actor and gifted writer, but drugs and alcohol quickly derailed his career. He spiraled downward. It took a decade of struggling with addiction before he found the strength to climb out of that black hole. Throughout that time, he still continued to write books and plays while working a variety of jobs, including at chain bookstores and adult theaters, as a bathroom attendant, and as a reporter. At one point, he went bankrupt attempting to make a film about Malcolm X.

One day in early 1990s Los Angeles, while recovering from his first heart attack, McGriff was reading a literary magazine. An article in the publication listed the four best writing programs in the country. Higher education was on his mind because a close friend had recently said to him that he would never get a real job without a degree. He had earned a music scholarship to Penn State but had dropped out before finishing his degree. He looked over the list and spotted the Iowa Writer's Workshop, which was located at the University of Iowa. A few pages later, McGriff saw an advertisement for Iowa State University. Not distinguishing between the two state schools, he sent his application to Iowa State and was accepted three weeks later. He didn't realize until later that he was heading to Iowa State University and not the University of Iowa.

When he arrived in 1994, simmering racial tensions on campus were getting ready to boil over. Local newspapers had been covering several stories, including a sit-in protest by the Black Student Alliance (BSA) over a professor's handling of an African American history class, a food service worker spotted with racist tattoos, the closing of a resource center for Hispanic students, and the student government's rejection to fund a Mr. and Ms. Black Pageant.

A dark cloud had also gathered over that year's VEISHEA. Both the 1988 and 1992 VEISHEAs had seen large student riots, and the school was considering ending the 70-year-old spectacle. Instead, given the racial tensions on campus, the planning committee decided that the 1994 VEISHEA would be a 100th anniversary celebration of George Washington Carver's graduation from Iowa State University. It was hoped that by focusing on honoring Carver and celebrating diversity, a third riot in six years could be avoided. Several events focused on the nobility of Carver's story. A torch relay from Carver's home in Missouri to Ames was created to highlight his journey. A musical honoring the scientist would be performed at the Memorial Union. The date was also pushed back to allow the cooler weather to calm the crowds.

Yet despite the university's attempts to keep the students under control, Campustown saw its ugliest riot of the 20th century. More than 2,000 students and spectators threw rocks and bottles at police officers and buildings. The crowd originally formed to protest the breaking up of off-campus parties during the event, but it soon morphed into an all-out melee. It grew so large and chaotic that the Ames police broke up the massive crowd with riot gear, shields, and tear gas. The black eye for the school detracted from an otherwise noble event meant to honor one of its, and the nation's, African American pioneers.

The following year, McGriff finished his undergraduate degree and stayed on at Iowa State for a master's in creative writing. His thesis would be based on a friend and Black Panther sentenced to death for the murder of a Philadelphia police officer and was titled, "Live from Death Row: This Is Mumia Abu-Jamal."

Resistance was a core belief of McGriff's. "I feel that the culture, and cultures do this, has equated Martin Luther King [Jr.] with nonviolence, but the phrase should be 'nonviolent resistance,'" he once told the *Philadelphia City Paper.* "He was about creating tension, about creating crisis, and he said so, in *Letter from a Birmingham Jail.* And that part has gotten lost." And it was resistance the led McGriff to help organize a movement on campus whose collateral damage would ignite Jack Trice's legacy.

**WHEN MARTIN JISCHKE** became Iowa State University's president in 1991, he inherited a ticking time bomb. It finally went off in 1995. Jischke was a physicist with a PhD in aeronautics and astronautics from MIT. He had grown up in a working-class Chicago family with five siblings. At a young age he took an interest in sales jobs and understood what it meant to sell to people. He honed his salesmanship throughout his life, and those skills became especially useful for fundraising. As he later told an interviewer at Purdue University, of which he would one day become president, "I have absolutely no fear of selling to anybody anything."

Jischke also learned at an early age he could outwork most people through grit and determination. Most people, he found, were not prepared to work as hard as he was. If someone stood in his way, his perseverance would wear them down. This idea became a recurring theme in his tenure at Iowa State. In the early years of his presidency, he became known for a single phrase: "You can't whine your way to the top."

As a former teacher, Jischke had a strong interest in student autonomy. But as an administrator, everyone needed to understand the limitations of their respective roles. While he felt students had the right to raise questions and even to disagree with him on issues, ultimately they did not run the university; he and those appointed to leadership did. If an official committee ruled on something, it became the final word.

The ticking time bomb that Jischke inherited came in the form of a building naming, but this time it wasn't for Jack Trice. Jischke's predecessor, interim president Milton Glick, had approved the naming of one of the oldest brick buildings on campus in honor of Carrie Chapman Catt. Catt, like Carver, was a celebrated alumnus of Iowa State. She worked alongside Susan B. Anthony for women's suffrage and was Anthony's handpicked successor to lead the National American Woman Suffrage Association.

In honor of Catt's accomplishments directed toward women's voting rights, several groups and individuals in Ames, including the League of Women Voters, lobbied for years to rename a building for her. In 1989 a petition was circulated to rename Old Botany Hall for Catt, who had left her entire estate to Iowa State University. The authors noted only a single potential objection to naming a campus building for Catt: It might be referred to derogatorily as the Cathouse. This alone, they said, should not be justification enough to block the proposition. They foresaw no other objections to their petition. The proposal passed through the official channels and was approved by the board of regents. The naming was announced in 1990 at a banquet featuring Catt historians, an Iowa State University Catt archivist, Catt supporters, and Catt's great-great-great-niece. It was meant to highlight Catt's strong female leadership and her contributions to feminist history.

However, there was one thing in Catt's past that the people who recognized her political accomplishments did not foresee as controversial. Whether intentional or not, and that would be debated, Catt's strategy for advancing women's voting rights had come dangerously close to, if not outright supporting, White supremacy. While campaigning in Southern states for women's suffrage, Catt had played on the fears of racial tension. She painted the support for women's voting rights as a tool to politically oppress Blacks and other minorities. Catt told audiences in South Carolina and Mississippi, "White supremacy will be strengthened, not weakened, by women's suffrage."

Her remarks disparaging minorities where not limited to just this one stump speech. At other times, for instance, she spoke of prohibiting voting by uneducated immigrants and referred to Indians as savages. At one point, she was quoted in the *Oregon Daily Journal* saying, "It is an absolute fabrication that I have at any time advocated marriage between the white and negro races. Furthermore, I believe it to be an absolute crime against nature." The first sentence of the quote was meant to counter attacks at the time from her political opponent asserting that she was also campaigning for integration. That was true. That was not on her platform of issues. But the meaning of her second sentence was less clear.

The question of the day became: Should Catt be honored for her significant historical contribution to women's rights in light of her purported disparaging attacks on other groups? Was she simply a product of her time that needed to be understood in the eyes of history, or was she just a blatant racist? Perhaps it was more nuanced than that. Were her quotes taken out of context, and were they in fact calculated to shield the burgeoning and fragile women's suffrage movement from being entangled with other controversial movements of the day that could drag it down? What, then, of Black women?

Where would they fall in a debate on supporting women's suffrage that also disenfranchised Black voters? If it had been 2020, the term "cancel culture" probably would have been thrown around. But in 1995, it became a debate that swept up Iowa State University.

Iowa State student Meron Wondwosen was studying abroad in Paris when she first learned of the Catt Hall naming controversy. She herself was a Black immigrant born in Ethiopia. Her family had lived in several African and European countries prior to immigrating to the United States when she was 12 years old. Wondwosen was a member of the Black Student Alliance and the editor in chief for the on-campus publication *UHURU* magazine, named after the Swahili word for "freedom." The magazine was funded by the Black Student Alliance and focused on issues affecting people of color on the Iowa State University campus through acts of "intelligent activism."

Following her take on the controversy, Wondwosen wrote an article in *UHURU* titled "The Catt Is Out of the Bag: Racism Within the Suffrage Movement." It was a five-page article referencing several books, but mostly *Daughters of Jefferson, Daughters of Bootblacks: Racism and American Feminism*, a 1986 book by Rutgers professor, theologian, and ethics scholar Barbara Hilkert Andolsen. Andolsen would later become Fordham's first chair in applied Christian ethics.

Using Andolsen's examples, Wondwosen agreed that Carrie Chapman Catt, Susan B. Anthony, and Elizabeth Cady Stanton were geniuses, intellectuals, and the "pulse of the suffrage movement," but she cautioned against painting "these women as paragons of virtue." Wondwosen took particular umbrage to a pamphlet for the upcoming naming festivities that referenced Catt's "glorious past." To Wondwosen, Catt's words had been anything but "perfection." It had to be recognized that Catt was human, and therefore fallible. Her story was being painted with too wide a brush.

Wondwosen described the initial support for abolition among the women's suffrage movement. But then she highlighted the fact that Frederick Douglass was asked not to attend the Southern conferences for women's suffrage, for it might have signaled support for the social equality of races. Wondwosen herself wrote, "It seems fair to say that in this instance the suffragists were caught between a rock and a hard place. Should they advocate for equality and vote for all and accomplish neither?" To her, the suffragists chose a shortcut and cut their Black supporters loose. If Black rights had weighed them down, then the 19th Amendment may never have happened. But in doing so, the suffragists "lowered themselves down to the level of bigots in an effort to attract supporters." One might wonder if the same could be said for those who abandoned Jack Trice in favor of the better-financed and easier-to-sell Cyclone Stadium.

Wondwosen's article was published on September 29, 1995, only a week before the naming of Catt Hall was scheduled. But it was enough time to stir up student concern and resentment. Despite the years of trickling progress at administrative meetings that had already occurred, the students felt they had never been given a say in the building naming. Those in support of Catt had followed the formal policies as they saw fit. But it was the sudden and emotional plea of the students that caught the campus's attention. Referencing the date of Wondwosen's article publication, the opposition would soon become known as the September 29th Movement.

IT WAS ON a cold, rainy Friday afternoon in October when Carrie Chapman Catt Hall was formally dedicated. The event took place in the Plaza of Heroines as part of Women's Week 1995. Catt's name would officially adorn both Catt Hall and the Carrie Chapman Catt Center for Women and Politics. Young members of Catt's sorority, Pi Beta Phi, dressed in clothing reminiscent of the 1880s and handed out programs to those seated in attendance. Jane Cox, a retired professor and former stage director for Iowa State University Theatre, as well as a strong Catt supporter, opened the ceremony.

"To consider the past and the present isn't enough," Cox said. "We must aim higher to see the truth more clearly and better respond to the rights of others."

A list of "saviors" who helped the $5 million project come to fruition was announced. Among those mentioned were community and campus activists who had saved the Old Botany Hall from demolition on three occasions and helped place the building on the National Register of Historic Places.

President Jischke then recognized those who had dedicated specific areas of the building. He leaned on quotes by both Martin Luther King Jr. and Robert F. Kennedy to illustrate the importance of each person's energy to make Catt Hall possible. "I am very proud to have Carrie Chapman Catt as part of Iowa State's history," Jischke said. "This building is a symbol of Iowa State's commitment to equality."

Jischke himself had lent a significant hand to supporting Catt Hall financially. When his predecessor did not become the permanent president, Jischke became stuck with finding the money for the planned renovations. He needed to find $5 million. He struggled to find enough donors but ultimately succeeded. It was something that would help shape his view of the controversy.

Iowa's lieutenant governor Joy Corning also spoke that day and concurred with the symbolism of Catt as a measure of women's progress. But she also challenged women to set new goals, saying they should "accept nothing less than flawless honesty and integrity" from themselves and others. She also thanked the men of Catt's day for voting for the 19th Amendment, for without them, women would not have had the right to vote. "Men reached a high level of wisdom that day," she said.

The day's festivities concluded with the Iowa State University band playing the alma mater's song "Bells of Iowa State" while members of the crowd sang along. Last, Jane Cox performed several scenes from her one-woman play about Catt titled *The Yellow Rose of Suffrage*.

ATTENDING THE WATERLOGGED ceremony that day was Celia Naylor-Ojurongbe, director of the Women's Center and an advisor for the Women's Week Committee. The day before the Catt Hall naming, she had participated in a forum called "Race, Ethnicity and Gender in the Suffrage Movement." The forum had been added during Women's Week in response to the recent discussion on campus regarding the relationship of the suffrage movement to racism. The session was held at noon in the Chautauqua Tent, which stood in the shadow of the soon-to-be-named Catt Hall.

There were three panelists for the event and one moderator. From her chair in the audience, she could discern little or no actual references during the presentations to race or racism in the suffrage movement. Finally, after more than an hour, while half of the audience was leaving, the topic of ethnicity was mentioned. Celia leaned forward in her chair and waited with interest to see where the conversation would go. Instead she flopped back in her chair, utterly disappointed as the discussion turned to the experiences of Irish and Irish American Catholic women.

She stood up and posed her own question about racism and ethnocentrism to the panelists. A brief discussion ensued but quickly died down. Not long after, someone brought up the question regarding Carrie Chapman Catt and the issue of race and racism. Naylor-

Ojurongbe felt her breath freeze, as seemingly did all the panelists. At first, no one spoke. Then most of the experts admitted that they were not knowledgeable enough about Carrie Chapman Catt specifically to make a statement on the issue. One panelist did offer up that she had, to some extent, read about Carrie Chapman Catt and could conclude there were "inconsistencies" in Carrie Chapman Catt's speeches: Much of Catt's tactics depended on which audience she was addressing.

Feeling that the question still lingered in the air, the moderator turned to the audience and asked Jane Cox if she could provide some input. After all, Cox had written her one-woman play about Catt. To Cox's credit, she had undertaken four years of research on Catt at a time when primary sources were often difficult to track down. Computer access was extremely limited. Her efforts required traveling both to the Library of Congress and the New York Public Library in her quest for primary documents. Notes had to be quickly scribbled onto pieces of paper and photocopies made on antiquated copy machines. Further, her research was done to honor, not condemn, Iowa State University's famous alum.

The audience had already thinned, as the session was scheduled to close in a few minutes. Cox began her well-intentioned response by first stating what she found to be the "dictionary definition" of the word *racism*. With that definition in mind, she stated, "Carrie Chapman Catt was not a racist," and she went on to defend this position.

When Naylor-Ojurongbe heard those words, she could not "even begin to articulate how much anger, frustration and disappointment" she felt. According to an op-ed she published soon after, she described that all she could think about in that moment was

> how in this time someone like Jane Cox could actually define racism by using a dictionary. I thought about what a privilege it is for someone to talk about, indeed to define, racism in all its

complexity with a simplistic definition offered by a dictionary. All the works that I have read on racism, all the classes I have taken on racism, all of the racist comments I have heard, flooded my mind, and yet for Jane Cox, as well as for others, the yard stick for defining a racist person was a dictionary's definition. What a privilege!

In her op-ed, she went on to address two examples of what Cox proposed as evidence of Catt's nonracism. To Naylor-Ojurongbe they were classic examples of skewed perspectives; they reflected the shaded justifications of inherent biases that purported to demonstrate the absence of racism.

The first was that Mary Church Terrell, the cofounder of the National Association of Colored Women, spoke of Catt as a friend in her autobiography. Cox had noted Terrell and Catt were colleagues for 30 years in the suffrage movement. In her biography, Terrell noted there was racism among suffragists but stopped short of naming any names. She did observe that the older suffragists were less racist than the younger generation. She also wrote that Carrie Chapman Catt was "without racial prejudice."

For Naylor-Ojurongbe, this argument fell into the "some of my best friends are Black" bucket, which ignores that even those people who have minority friends may not demonstrate racism toward their friends but can still be racist at some level. Naylor-Ojurongbe described it thusly in her op-ed:

> I am not going to offer all the details about why this kind of thinking has been, is and will continue to be flawed. However, I hope that you will consider that merely because a European-American woman created a friendship with an African-

American woman, or with several African-American women, the European-American woman could still be racist against other members of the African-American community. She could still hold racist views about African-American people in general; she could still perceive African Americans as being less than or innately inferior to herself and to European-Americans in general; she could still express racist views in her interactions with African Americans; and she could bring all of those views with her when she sits and drinks tea with her African-American woman friend.

Cox, on the other hand, felt the relationship between the women went far beyond the "some of my best friends are Black" category. The second argument that did not sit well with Naylor-Ojurongbe was that Catt's activism involved people from countries all over the world. She felt this was yet another flawed argument. In this case, she wrote, someone who is interested in helping people who live in countries outside the United States could also simultaneously remain racist toward people of color living in her own country.

But even despite what she saw as flawed arguments being made in support of Catt's words, something else broke Naylor-Ojurongbe's heart even more. It occurred at the end of Cox's comments. All the remaining audience members, including fellow members of the Women's Week and forum planning committee, enthusiastically clapped in support of her comments as if the matter had been cleared up and easily settled. It was far from so.

Women's Week 1995 came to a conclusion. Catt Hall was officially named. But minorities on the faculty such as Naylor-Ojurongbe and Black students such as Wondwosen were left feeling both unseen and unheard. The controversy, however, was not over. The media had begun to take hold of the story and cover it at a national level.

In an interview with the *New York Times*, Jischke said, "While I don't support everything that Carrie Chapman Catt did or said, I believe her contribution to women's suffrage and world peace are worthy of the recognition that the university has given her."

The president of the Ames chapter of the NAACP publicly disagreed with the decision. "The university needs to publicly acknowledge that sometimes good people can do bad things," President George Jackson told the *Times*. He suggested that the university should be more one-sided when it came to perceived issues of racism. It should change the name of Catt Hall, which would clearly send the message, "I will not tolerate racism in any form or fashion."

RACISM AND A Black football players were topics on the nightly news, across dinner tables, and at office water coolers across the country during the late 1990s, but it had nothing to do with Jack Trice. Rather, it was because of the O.J. Simpson murder trial. On October 3, 1995, newly hired Iowa State University assistant dean of students and BSO adviser Terri Houston was scheduled to give a talk titled "Everything You Wanted to Know About Blacks and Whites but Were Afraid to Ask." She had been brought to Iowa State to promote diversity and support student advocacy. Houston had previously served in minority affairs at several other universities, but what she saw on the campus of Iowa State when she arrived was "a different kind of advocacy," and it was everywhere. It was palpable. And she loved it—mostly because she loved to see people engaged, especially students.

On the day the Simpson verdict was to be announced, Houston and the manager of the M-Shop, who like Houston was Black, set up a big screen to watch the outcome. As word of the impending verdict spread, the room filled up with mostly White students. The nation collectively held its breath when the court clerk finally read the verdict: not guilty. As O.J. smiled and hugged his lawyers, there was an eerie silence in the Machine Shop. No one said anything. No one moved.

*Damn*, was all Houston could think. She could see the White students were numb. She heard murmurs and mumbles as the students filed back out just as quickly as they had come in. She turned to the manager, who was sitting next to her. She thought she heard her mutter "Yes!" under her breath. Houston, whose job it was to work on race relations and diversity, could see the trial verdict already playing right into the dynamics of race on campus.

Just as the winter and snow were arriving, the September 29th Movement was heating up. That fall they had proclaimed their mission was the "elimination of racism, xenophobia, sexism, homophobia, and classism at Iowa State University." In February 1996 a large group of students and faculty met at the Black Cultural Center on campus to discuss strategy. The group's main focus was to change the name of Catt Hall. They decided to start a letter-writing campaign. More than 1,000 students and faculty signed letters addressed to Jischke. The next month, in a public display of their unity, more than a hundred students and faculty silently marched in the bitter cold dressed in all black. They were led by McGriff, Wondwosen, and fellow Black graduate student Allan Nosworthy. Nosworthy is most remembered for going on a hunger strike to support the movement.

The protesters marched to the steps of Catt Hall, where the three student leaders stood in front of them. "Fists up!" they called to the crowd as Black Power salutes shot into the air. "Fists down!" they cried.

Wondwosen read a prepared speech in front of the huddled local TV reporters, which included him saying, "The naming of this building after Catt condones the methods she used to push her political agenda."

It was already well-known that Catt's political strategy was being debated among members of the Iowa State community. But it was Wondwosen's next statement that stood at the core of the September 29th Movement: "Changing the name of Catt Hall will show a concern on the university's part that includes the interests and issues of non-majority groups on this campus."

The national media attention of Catt Hall continued and began to include coverage of the September 29th Movement's demands. Fourteen NAACP chapters called for the renaming of Catt Hall while 26 of the 27 female Iowa legislators supported keeping the name in an open letter. Even Jesse Jackson, who swung by Iowa State University as part of a voter registration campaign, weighed in on the subject. He first provided the usual caveat that many commentators from outside of campus admitted before making a comment, namely that he had not studied the specific issue. But he said if racism was used to swing votes in favor of ratifying the amendment, then "the end does not justify the means."

But he also recalled his own struggle to rectify Thomas Jefferson as an important founding father who also owned slaves and had a Black mistress. Rev. Jackson had found it easier to come to terms with Jefferson's past and embrace his achievements by looking to Jefferson's later statements calling slavery morally wrong. Memories could be redeemable if the transgressors themselves had evolved.

The conflict between the supporters and detractors of Catt had also reached the school faculty. Derrick Rollins had been an engineering professor at Iowa State University long enough to reach tenure. During his time at the university, at least from his perspective, "people got along well." He felt very comfortable at work, on campus, and in the surrounding community. For years he had coached teams throughout Iowa, and often he and his daughter were the only African American people on the field. Yet he felt "very much accepted." Nevertheless, some of those feelings changed when McGriff, Wondwosen, and Nosworthy showed up to his office one day unannounced.

The three September 29th Movement leaders wanted to talk to him regarding his influence and recent appointment to the president's cabinet. Rollins had been asked to serve as Jischke's adviser on diversity. Prior to that day, he and the three graduate students had not crossed paths before simply because English and engineering were on separate sides of the campus. They had come to him to discuss Catt Hall and the September 29th Movement. After hearing the students talk, Rollins found he could relate to what they were feeling. It was a feeling of not being seen, of not being heard. After that initial conversation, members of the movement would continue to come back to his office several other times and leave papers and other notes for him to read.

Intrigued by what he learned from the group, Rollins also started his own research into Catt, although he was limited in some of the resources he could access from campus. In September 1996, after considering what he could access and what he heard from the students, Rollins wrote a memo that he believed "changed the game." He directed the memo to Jischke and copied every member of the cabinet and every dean in the school.

In the memo, Rollins called for renaming Catt Hall. He understood her contribution as a great woman of history and the importance of the school having accepted money from donors. Yet, he wrote, the minority students' "perception should be honored with sensitivity, respect, and understanding. Hence, the issue is no longer whether

Catt was politically racist, but whether members of the September 29th Movement are significant enough to really matter." Rollins stressed that the perception the students had of keeping the Catt Hall name was important because "it is this perception that makes them feel insignificant, unwanted, and mistreated…it makes them question their true acceptance on this campus."

He proposed an alternative. He suggested that the administration move the multicultural programs out of Catt Hall because the administration's vision of Catt Hall did not coincide with that of people of color. There was a conflict of belief, and he stated, "You can't just bring someone into your celebration and expect them to celebrate the same way."

Rollins thought the administration demonstrated naivete. If they truly wanted to create a campus that welcomed all people, including people of color, their symbols needed to represent all members of the Iowa State community. A sense of equality and sensitivity was missing. "When you say you want to change the environment, the true test is not how you ultimately feel," Rollins later recalled. "It's how the other people who enter that environment feel."

To him, what the September 29th Movement was doing was no different from what other students had done at Iowa State University. The university had always been a place of protests and free speech exercises, and the 1990s were no different. What was different this time, though, was that these students now had an ally with direct access to the university president in Rollins. And he felt exactly the same way they did about the issue.

In private and openly, Rollins felt that he could speak freely because Jischke wasn't his boss. The chairs of the colleges were his superiors. Most vice presidents in the room where cabinet decisions were made reported directly to Jischke. Rollins didn't have that problem. He could speak his mind without fear of retribution. In fact, he and Jischke had discussed that if an impasse ever did come about, they would just part ways and Rollins would just go back to teaching, because he had tenure. Often several people in the cabinet meetings would tell Rollins privately that they agreed with his take on the controversy but couldn't speak up publicly. However, as the weeks and months passed, Rollins noticed others becoming more emboldened to speak their minds on the matter to Jischke.

Rollins felt the public nature of his memo created a lot of problems for Jischke. It became clear that Rollins was now a very visible advocate for the students, something that didn't sit well with many of the more powerful university supporters. They didn't like the optics. In a significant backlash to his memo, several prominent members of Iowa State University and its alumni called for his resignation. Rollins didn't back down. He saw what he was doing as bringing an issue to the forefront that they all had to face. He was stirring the pot and felt that was a good thing. In his opinion, the university needed to do something about recognizing the voice of students of color. At first, it wasn't Jack's name going on a building he sought but Catt's name coming *off*.

Soon after, several minority faculty members, including Rollins and Houston, set up a meeting between themselves, Jischke, and members of the September 29th Movement. It was meant to be an open discussion, a negotiation of sorts. Given the charged atmosphere, a moderator was suggested. Jischke turned down a moderator and decided the meeting would happen behind closed doors. Other attempts at open discussions on the issues would end with students crashing Jischke's presidential breakfasts or organizing unofficial town halls that resulted in trespassing charges.

Houston sat at the conference table serving multiples roles, including student advisor and advocate as well as cochair of the Black faculty group. As a faculty member and woman of color, she knew she was standing in the middle of a contentious circumstance. The meeting focused on the September 29th Movement. McGriff and Wondwosen were among those invited to the discussion. Jischke wanted to know what the students actually were looking for. With all their protests and activism, what did they ultimately want to see happen? What was their endgame? The student answer was straightforward: Catt's name should not adorn a building on their campus.

The exchanges that took place were intense and heated. Houston was in the middle of taking copious notes when Jischke stopped and turned to his right. He asked her if she was recording something. Was she taking notes that were going to be brought outside the meeting? Jischke said he would not continue the discussion if she continued to take notes. She replied she would continue taking notes, which resulted in another contentious back-and-forth. Jischke made it clear he would not change his position and left the meeting, leaving the same questions lingering in the air. Student and faculty concerns regarding the renovation of the Black Cultural Center, the school's ethnic studies program, and retention-recruitment of minority students were left on the table. There would be no resolution that day.

"The Black faculty and staff were fearful for their jobs," Houston thought. They wanted to know how to support the minority students and their campaign. Many were torn between advocating for something they believed in as minorities themselves and keeping their jobs. Houston believed her mission was "creating a safe space for students to express their views," but she struggled to find the right balance between professional and ethical obligations.

Another member of the September 29ᵗʰ Movement grappled with his own relationship to Jischke. Kyle Pierce had come to Iowa State on a George Washington Carver scholarship. During his freshman year, Pierce was involved in a presidential leadership program. Part of the program involved meeting with Jischke and his wife at their house. Pierce and his co-leaders represented a relative cross-section of Iowa State University students, and they brought their own unique perspectives to the discussion.

Jischke seemed approachable to Pierce. His thoughts seemed student-centric—at least at first. As time went on and Pierce became president of the Black Student Alliance, he felt Jischke became less receptive to minority students. Their causes and activism no longer interested him. In fact, they seemed to be a burden.

Rather than meet with them in person, Jischke would send people on his behalf. He tried to use Black administrators to bridge the communication gap. Many of them did their job well. For example, Pierce liked talking with Houston and Rollins. But it became a little too obvious and condescending when others were hired who seemed less receptive to the students. The term Uncle Tom was sometimes thrown around.

Pierce and many of the Black students felt isolated. Many of them had arrived from outside Iowa to find little to no support system available. They were kids from large urban areas and inner cities such as Chicago and Detroit. They weren't expecting the racial makeup in Ames to be the same as where they had come from, but they were expecting "a healthy environment for people of color." Some mentors, such as George Jackson, had been advocating for minority students for decades and became a father figure to many. But still programs such as the Black Cultural Center continued to be severely underfunded.

Black students and educators understood there was an entire world beyond campus where minorities continued to struggle with high rates of unemployment, poverty, imprisonment, and death. Many of them knew people who had been shot or imprisoned, or who were begging for money on the streets. Referencing the 1995 Million Man March in an interview with the *Daily*, Derrick Rollins pointed out that Iowa State University and its students should be concerned about the problems of African American men, saying, "If we continue on this path, it's going to be very destructive for all Americans." Students of all colors from Iowa State University would have to go out into the world and deal with these issues that would test every American head-on.

By September 1996 the members of the September 29th Movement had been fighting to be heard for a year. Milton McGriff continued to be one of the loudest and most unique voices. Several students would follow him around wearing black berets and dark sunglasses. They were his Black Panthers–style security. Many stood behind him motionless at rallies, including one on the one-year anniversary of the movement's inception. He was teaching them lifelong lessons on how to be an activist.

On September 29 Milton arranged for a very public spectacle. He would debate Jane Cox on the Catt Hall issue live on the airwaves of campus radio station KURE-FM. It wasn't their first debate. In fact, they had actually known each other for some time. They first met when McGriff was a student in Cox's 300-level playwriting class while completing his undergraduate degree.

During her writing course, Cox emphasized to her students the importance of writing and then rewriting. Each student would read his or her first draft and then their subsequent rewrites aloud. Each time there would be group discussion and editing suggestions. To Cox, McGriff's initial script was far better than the other students' in the class, but each time he read it aloud, he was unwilling to change it. He would argue with even the smallest suggestion, such as simply reversing the order of two words in a single line. Listening was not one of his strengths, she thought then. Nevertheless, Cox made an effort to be patient with him. She thought he must have felt awkward being surrounded by younger students and faculty.

They would often meet after class once everyone else had left. With the two of them alone, he would vent his anger about a variety of topics, including capitalism, police brutality, the neglect of Mao's teachings among the Black community, and the disrespect of its revolutionaries. Cox would mostly listen, but sometimes she responded. As the semester went on, the intensity of his objections and their occasional debates seemed to grow. But when the end of the semester came, she thought they had parted ways with mutual respect for each other. She thought they were destined to walk separate paths. But all that changed, she felt, with Catt Hall.

Cox felt attacked, both figuratively and literally. Things felt especially personal when she was leaving theater rehearsal and heading to her car late one night. She always parked in the same spot behind Pearson Hall outside a large rehearsal room. When she came out of rehearsal that night, she stopped dead in her tracks. Someone had taken a sledgehammer to her car. The front fender on the driver's side was smashed inward with repeated blows. The same thing had happened to the car of another faculty member who sided with her on the Catt Hall debate. They found it difficult to believe these were random acts.

While Cox was feeling targeted by the September 29th Movement, Pierce felt like he and the other Black students of the movement were still being ignored. To Cox, they seemed to have a powerful grip on campus. To Pierce, they were being tossed aside. The Big 12 conference on Black student government was approaching, and Pierce was in charge of the planning committee. Jischke called him into his office and told him if the September 29ᵗʰ Movement would stop protesting and making a ruckus, he would give Pierce the $20,000 he had requested for the event. It was clear Jischke just wanted to move on from the whole thing. Pierce didn't know what to say. He felt that Jischke was offering him a payoff. He refused the offer.

Behind the scenes Derrick Rollins, who still had the president's ear, continued to talk with Jischke. Jischke valued that Rollins was not only Black but had also grown up in the inner city and had risen from his own community to reach a high level of academic achievement. Rollins had built a reputation for working with a number of unrepresented groups through his own initiatives in the STEM fields, including with both Black and female students.

Rollins and Jischke both recognized that a lot of work needed to be done to lift up underrepresented students. Rollins felt Iowa State was sincerely involved in doing that, especially in the sciences. The school had no choice but to recognize the problem because it so strongly stood out. The numbers of underrepresented students were so low that the board of regents created a mandate to increase the number of minority students. For years the school had continued to struggle to achieve the mandate, but under Jischke the needle was moving. He needed to keep the momentum going in the right direction. He couldn't afford to have Black students standing on the corners of the campus telling prospective minority students on the campus tour not to go there, or people such as McGriff publishing open letters to the freshmen about the dire racial situation at the school.

Rollins realized Jischke was facing two groups at Iowa State University who were unhappy: women and people of color. Each was facing discrimination in its own way. Rollins agreed Catt should be honored for her work, but she still needed to be framed in the right light. That meant she wasn't a hero for all people. Iowa State needed a different hero—someone who could make the university a home for both Black and White students. He thought maybe Jack Trice was that hero.

Rollins knew Jischke well and that renaming Catt Hall was off the table. The president had already made his thoughts on the matter well-known. After reading Catt's speech in question, Jischke had concluded that Catt was not a racist. He felt that if the entire speech were read carefully, she was making a statement of fact, not a political statement. It was true what she had said to the Southerners. So he decided he would not change the name of the building, or at least he would make no recommendation to the board of regents.

Jischke felt most people were waiting and watching to see how he would decide on the Catt Hall issue. As a university president, he had realized that issues of race, gender, and sexual orientation were so intensely personal and so incendiary to a community that very few people really wanted to join in the debate. Most preferred watching from the sideline, even though privately they had their own opinions. Jischke felt it had become an argument between him and a group of students. It began to feel like a lonely battle.

Jischke surmised that the vast majority of the Iowa State University community just wished the debate would go away. A large percentage of the minority community was sympathetic to the students and also wanted the name changed. At the same time, a large number of the women in the majority saw the Catt debate as a symbol for a longer struggle in the recognizing of women's rights. It was a struggle they too didn't want to lose.

Even if the students were right—and Jischke didn't think they were—he thought "Catt had been such a remarkable political leader and such a distinguished alum of the university that when taken as a whole, her life was exemplary."

He would later tell an interviewer at Purdue University, "To dismiss all those accomplishments and unravel a decision that had been taken by the governing board that involved lots of donors contributing to the naming of this building, and had done very publicly and very openly, I thought was a mistake, and I worried about the intolerance that was in the students' view of all of this. The kind of arrogance of youth that one mistake was enough to condemn a person."

Jischke turned to the lessons of Gandhi and the lessons of Martin Luther King Jr. on forgiveness, saying, "Forgiveness is the ultimate moral authority, and the students didn't understand that." And if lessons on forgiveness didn't clear it up for them, he said, "these kinds of issues are ultimately decided by the governing board and the properly appointed president, that the students don't run the university."

With the case closed in his mind, Jischke came up with a plan for alternatives. One proposal was moving multicultural studies out of Catt Hall and into Carver Hall as Rollins had suggested. Another was a program offering 100 full-tuition scholarships and a support system for students of color in Iowa. Rollins told Jischke that wouldn't be enough. They needed to honor people of color in a way that was on the same magnitude as naming a building. Something like, say, a stadium.

Naming something brought in money, he said. Catt Hall had brought in donations through many smaller amounts that ultimately added up. Football was a much larger stage. The Jack Trice movement had never gone away. Unlike in the 1970s and 1980s, the Black students weren't joining with the Jack Trice Memorial Stadium Committee to call for the stadium to be named for Jack. And unlike in the early 1990s, Black athletes were now being discouraged from getting involved in the protests. But there were still students, both Black and White, who brought up Jack's name.

GSB president Adam Gold had recently made the renaming of the stadium part of his campaign platform and had spoken to two of the regents through a student both parties knew. All indications as far as he could tell were that the regents would approve the name change—but only if Jischke himself recommended it. The GSB passed its own resolution calling for the stadium to be named for Jack. Even the official committee responsible for naming buildings, the one whose decision had bound President Parks for so long, had changed its mind. It was no longer the committee's official recommendation that Jack be denied the honor. Once again the tremors of the Jack Trice Memorial Stadium Committee could be felt underneath the campus.

As Jack's name began to resurface, Rollins began to bring up the issue at cabinet meetings. He would talk about it in private with other members of the faculty. He also approached newly appointed vice president Tom Hill, who also was African American, with the idea. The two of them agreed now was the time to name the stadium for Jack. But just deciding on it wasn't enough. When they thought about it more, Jack's name alone probably wasn't going to be a mega-draw for donors. And the Black alumni population was scant. The students were still pushing for the name, but even after decades of relative progress, Rollins feared that big-money donors still didn't want a Black man's name on the side of their stadium. Maybe they were foolish in suggesting it to Jischke.

For Rollins and many in his circle, naming the stadium wasn't about politics. It wasn't about quelling student protests. It was about doing the right thing. Rollins had come to Iowa State to do research and teach engineering, not to become a cultural activist. He wasn't a social person by nature. He would have been happy with a quiet life of research. But when he saw the events around him unfolding, he felt a sense of responsibility come over him. Only a handful of other faculty members were stepping up, and they didn't know Jischke like he did. This wasn't the faculty of Charles Sohn, who had left Iowa State several years earlier. It wasn't the activists of the 1970s trying to stick it to the man. It was about people of color wanting to feel respected, heard, and seen.

Rollins saw a side of Jischke few others had seen. Even though they had disagreed on many topics, Jischke always listened to him. Rollins felt that Jischke's actions weren't driven by politics but rather by conscience. Sure, he was intelligent and direct, which often came across as intimidating. But in their private conversations, Rollins saw a tender person; he knew Jischke as someone who cared.

As a fellow engineer, Rollins knew Jischke was also an engineer at heart. Engineers calculated the numbers on *everything*. The students clearly still supported naming the stadium for Jack, but according to the latest information from Jischke's advisors, the alumni were still split 50–50. Many of the alumni felt that they had already recognized Jack and there was no need to recognize him further. Rollins was worried Jischke would see the money wasn't there. The numbers weren't adding up in Jack's favor.

Still Rollins pressed on. He began to bring up the idea more frequently in his meetings with Jischke. He turned up the pressure on the president. If Jischke wasn't doing anything about the Catt Hall situation, then he should at least do something to honor Trice. Jischke soon felt the pressure building from Rollins and others around him and realized he needed to act. He announced he would take some time to think about the Jack Trice situation and come to a decision. When he and Rollins met in early 1997, much to Rollins's surprise,

Jischke decided he would buck the numbers. He told Rollins he would approve renaming the stadium for Jack Trice.

Jischke had settled on a strategy of balance. He would try and even the scales in honoring Iowa State University's heroes. Rather than renaming Catt Hall, he would rename the stadium. While some may have found it pandering, Rollins found it honorable. He could see what ultimately drove Jischke was a passion for being a good person with a high moral base. He looked for the solution that allowed him to be true to himself but not compromise his position as an administrator. Renaming the stadium allowed him to do that. When Jischke finally agreed to the change, all Rollins thought to himself, as did so many who had come before him, was, *It's about time.*

Before coming to his final recommendation, Jischke said he met with several people, including Allen Boller, who had worked with Jack in the school's old gym. Boller was more than 90 years old but still remembered Jack as one of the "most gentlemanly" people he had ever met. Jack was always looking for ways to help others. When Jischke asked him what he thought of naming the stadium for Trice, Boller replied, "I think it's a terrific idea. I know where Jack is, and I think he'll like it too."

On February 20, 1997, President Jischke officially recommended to the board of regents that the football stadium at Iowa State University be named for Jack Trice. No name should accompany the field. It should just be Jack Trice Stadium. "Universities have precious few opportunities to recognize heroic qualities," he said. "This is one of those opportunities."

He followed up, "It is clear that Jack Trice, for a large majority of the students and others associated with Iowa State University, exemplifies a number of heroic qualities, including determination, courage, enthusiasm, and giving one's all to an important cause." He declared Jack Trice a hero, not so much for what he did with his short life but more so for what he represented.

In the press, even ex-president Parks supported the notion, stating that his original reservations were no longer relevant. "It's quite clear to me that a considerable majority think this is an appropriate thing, a good thing to do," he told the *Des Moines Register*.

A motion was brought forth to rename the stadium for Jack. Regent Nancy Pellet remarked that she had received a number of calls objecting to renaming the stadium for Jack, more calls than for any other issue before. She said the objections were not because of Jack Trice as a person or his race. Those who objected did so because to them changing the name would remove some of the ownership the alumni felt they had over the stadium. She said the stadium was built by selling it seat by seat. Many of the alumni felt that taking away the name Cyclone Stadium would remove their sense of ownership. Although she didn't specifically describe it that way, some may have heard her saying a group of alumni still felt the stadium was their house, not Jack's. Other regents agreed that not all of the alumni were buying into the idea.

Regent Ellengray Kennedy noted a call from an alumnus who had attended in the 1970s. At that time, the caller had been a student who supported the Jack Trice movement. Now the student had graduated to alumnus status and was thankful the renaming for Jack was finally happening. This served as an example of how the former members of the movement had now begun to grow into the alumni ranks.

A few of the regents remarked they weren't sure the students really wanted the stadium name changed. The numbers, however, told a different story. A recent poll on campus showed nearly 70 percent favored Jack Trice Stadium. Jischke also pointed out a poll of student-athletes: 85 percent of them wanted the stadium named for Jack. The students had spoken, and they had said the same thing for 25 years. The final statement of the night came from regent Jim Arenson. He thought the renaming was a great idea and fully supported it. He also remarked, "This is something that we are 30 to 40 years late in doing."

The vote that had been decades in the making finally began: the decision to name a major college football stadium after an African American athlete. It was the first of its kind. Despite the long fight, the gravity of the decision wasn't fully realized. Perhaps most in attendance didn't realize no other school had ever done it before. The motion was made, and the regents voted in turn.

The votes came in at 7–2 in favor. The motion was approved. Jack Trice's name would adorn the top of the Iowa State University football stadium, becoming the first and still only major college football stadium to honor an African American. Few people in the room realized history had been made. Or that so many people would find inspiration for decades to come from a decision made at a board of regents meeting in the middle of the country. Jack and his family mattered. They were seen. They were heard. They were honored. Jack also shared the newspaper headlines that day with another African American pioneer: The USTA announced that the U.S. Open tennis stadium in New York City would be named for Arthur Ashe.

WORD SPREAD ACROSS campus, and the new stadium name took effect immediately, but as it was winter, the official dedication would wait until the fall football season. Many reveled in the victory. They were young and old, children and parents—generations linked by a common cause. It was a fight that had lasted two and a half decades. Jack Trice, a "poor dead Black kid" whose grandparents were slaves and whose parents had fought to better their lives as Black people struggling in a White world, had lived up to his letter. He had done great things. He indeed had honored his race and his family.

But as in each step of the way before, it was not a victory without some detraction. There were always people who felt each victory rang somewhat hollow. It wasn't the honoring of Jack that they disparaged. He deserved it without question. It wasn't about Jack. It was about the way that the movement finally won. Several members of the September 29th Movement felt the naming was a tone-deaf gesture. Naming the stadium for Jack should have been a given. It shouldn't have taken so long and certainly shouldn't have required so much chaos to make it happen.

Pierce read about the name change in the student paper. While he felt it may have been a politically motivated decision, he agreed it was long overdue and Jack was well deserving of a lasting legacy. Although there was never any direct proof, Pierce, like many others, believed Jack was probably targeted that day on the football field because he was Black. Whether that was exactly true or not didn't matter. At the end of the day, Jack was still living life as a Black man in 1923, and if the September 29th Movement was helpful in honoring Jack's sacrifice almost 75 years later, then he was proud to be a part of it.

Wondwosen, who was by then president of the Black Student Alliance, was invited to be a part of the ceremony but refused. Her fight—their fight—was not over. She had several reservations about the ceremony. First, as far as she could tell, no minority student organizations were asked to be part of the planning committee, including the Black Student Alliance. Second, none of those organizations were even invited to the actual event. Only after Wondwosen and several other minority student leaders voiced their concerns did they receive an email invitation fewer than 48 hours before the dedication. Wondwosen saw this as a predictable, reactive move on the part of the administration.

She acknowledged the struggle to name the stadium for Jack stretched over decades and was supported by individuals of varied backgrounds, all united to ensure that a student-athlete of African descent was properly honored for his contribution to Iowa State University both on and off the field. But Wondwosen had a message to those who considered the late 1990s to have been a more "enlightened" time than the 1960s or '70s.

"Let us be frank," she wrote in a letter published by the *Daily* before the stadium naming. "The decision to dedicate the stadium after Jack Trice came about as a result of the efforts of the Black Student Alliance and the September 29th Movement."

These two organizations, she pointed out, had raised concerns about the lack of multiculturalism and diversity at Iowa State University, including the question of dedicating Catt Hall. They had called for increased funding for cultural studies programs and increased retention and recruitment of minority students, faculty, and staff. In so doing, she believed they had given the university "bad publicity."

"And so the decision to dedicate the stadium to Jack Trice was meant as an appeasement," she wrote. "But even in attempting to appease us, the administration cannot help excluding non-majority students from participating in this event. It is in their nature. It happened with the naming and dedication of Catt Hall and it is happening now with Jack Trice."

She did not wish for her participation and that of the BSA to give the impression or optics that students of color had a role in the dedication. She refused "to be a token."

She closed her letter with: "If you didn't know, now you know. The options are limited: remain invisible, become a sellout or a token or join the struggle! *La Lucha continua!*"

McGriff, in his own *Daily* op-ed on the subject, described the September 29th Movement as tree shakers: "We shake the tree, fruit falls to the ground and others pick it up," he wrote. "In our view, if no one shakes the tree, President Jischke—who thinks it's his tree—will dispense the fruit whenever he feels like it, if he feels like it at all."

McGriff described the tree shakers of the 1970s, and then the 1980s, who supported the stadium naming for Jack. Then along came the September 29th Movement. Although they did not actively campaign to get the stadium named for Jack, they too shook the tree.

He concluded, "The September 29th Movement likes to think we created a climate that allowed the stadium name change to happen."

FALL ARRIVED, AND with it the first official football season at Jack Trice Stadium. It was a momentous occasion. Students and football fans were greeted by signs declaring the new name: Jack Trice Stadium. This time the billboards and signs weren't erected by a ragtag group of agitators from the Jack Trice Memorial Stadium Committee. They were official Iowa Department of Transportation signs. From his desk, Don Kaul reacted to the decision with his usual dry brand of humor. "You people have rocket scientists at Iowa State," he sarcastically tapped out on his black typewriter. "You think you'd have figured it out long before now. It's nice to see it happen."

Almost 74 years after Jack passed away, the football stadium at Iowa State University was named for him. August 30, 1997, was declared Jack Trice Day at Iowa State. That afternoon, before the official stadium dedication ceremony, the statue of Jack was also rededicated. This time it wasn't Don Kaul but rather President Jischke at the helm of the ceremony. The statue, which had been located in the center of campus, was moved to a new location near the northeast entrance of the stadium.

Jischke spoke about Jack's sacrifice. One of the attendees listening was Robert Fisher. Fisher was the one who first noticed Jack wasn't sitting with the rest of the team in the segregated dining hall practically a lifetime earlier. Jischke pointed out they were not there today to focus on the tragedy of Jack's sudden passing. Instead they were honoring the inspiration Jack provided.

Jischke spoke about the students and supporters who had kept Jack's memory alive for more than 40 years after the dusty plaque was rediscovered in State Gym. He told of how the students of the 1970s, '80s, and '90s had fought to honor Jack, and how he was proud to be part of that movement (others may have disagreed). He rightfully pointed out that Jack Trice meant different things to different people. Harkening back to Jill Wagner's argument to the regents 20 years earlier, he declared Jack Trice a hero. He closed with a quote by Maya Angelou: "A great soul never dies. It brings us together again and again."

Also in attendance, standing near Jischke, was Gene Smith, Iowa State's first Black athletic director. Like Jack, his journey had brought him from the urban football fields of Cleveland to the farmlands of Iowa. His journey would soon take him back to Ohio, where *Black Enterprise* would name him one of the "50 most powerful African-Americans in sports." Jack helped to make that happen.

Smith could only describe the moment seeing Jack honored at such a high level as "emotional." He understood that at its most simple level, the moment of the naming represented the product of a great passion and years of work by student leaders. But to him, Jack represented something even deeper. Jack represented someone with honor and dignity who, as an athlete, made the ultimate sacrifice.

Gene recognized in Jack his understanding that if he failed as a Black man, there wouldn't be any opportunities for others who followed.

Being a part of the naming became one of the most important experiences of Smith's career. The symbolic nature of having an African American honored as the namesake of a major football stadium conjured up deep emotions for Smith. It was a time when the story of a person of color was no longer overlooked. Instead it called out for attention and was seen.

The evening of the stadium dedication was a clear but humid night in Ames. After planting the seeds and tending the garden for decades, the movement to rename the stadium in honor of Jack Trice had finally come to fruition. What had started out as a freshman English class project had ended in a historic moment for college football.

The official pregame dedication ceremony began, stretching back across a century to Jack's beginnings—through the turbulence of the 1960s and '70s, two World Wars, and a pandemic—to the beginning of the 20th century. With a voice booming from the public address system and across generations, the game announcer recalled the events leading up to Jack's tragic death.

Gladys Nortey, a star track-and-field athlete from Iowa State University who had spoken up during the 1990s to honor Jack's memory, took the microphone. As a Black female athlete, Nortey looked up to Jack, she said. He was as an inspiration. She looked down at the copy of Jack's letter she held in her hands three-quarters of a century after he had written it. She had been selected to read the letter to a crowd of nearly 44,000 gathered in attendance. Even more listened on the radio. At the time, Nortey felt that Black leaders at Iowa State were still limited, and for that reason she wanted to "stand tall in his honor." Jack's sacrifice for Iowa State University athletics was a legacy she could not forget. The crowd was silent as she read the letter. She concluded, "Be on your toes every minute if you expect to make good. Jack."

The Iowa State University band played "The Battle Hymn of the Republic" from the field. This time they didn't need to wear armbands. The celebration was out in the open, and the person they supported was clear. The crowd cheered. Black banners had been hung on both sides of the stadium before the dedication. In unison, the banners were folded inward and then dropped, revealing big, bright red letters beneath them. Emblazoned across the side of the stadium were the words that took decades to materialize: JACK TRICE STADIUM.

"Ladies and gentlemen, welcome to Jack Trice Stadium!" yelled the announcer. Jack had a name. It was not erased. Rather, it was painted on the side of the stadium. His story mattered, and so did those around him.

# Acknowledgments

I WOULD LIKE TO THANK JACK AND HIS FAMILY. IT WAS THEIR SACRIFICE that inspired generations after them. Many thanks to the students and faculty who never gave up the fight to honor Jack's legacy.

I am deeply indebted to those who wrote and published about Jack and his legacy before me, including Tom Emmerson, Steve Jones, Dorothy Schweider, and Jaime Schultz.

Thank you to those who agreed to answer questions or contribute to the book, including Charles Sohn, Milton McGriff (before he passed away so suddenly), Jane Cox, Bill Walsh, Michael Seemuth, Jill Wagner (and her scrapbook), Rick Yoder, Ed Freeman, Jim Smith, Stevan deProsse, Celia Naylor, Terri Rickers, Mike Keller, Chris Bennett, Dan Rice, Peggy Anderson, Peter Harris, Mark Carlson, Gladys Nortey, Derrick Rollins, Kyle Pierce, and Terri Houston. Thank you to Seneca Wallace and Eugene Smith for their forewords and forshining a light on Jack and his importance to their own careers.

I am indebted to the wonderful librarians and historians who helped gather materials on Jack and his story, including Olivia Hoge at the Cleveland Public Library; Tim Hudak, Kevin Gray at the Reed Library, Todd Michney, Russ Maurer, Bob Tangney at the Seattle Public Library, Lisa Labovitch and Larry O'Donnell in Everett, Rachael Altman, Brian Shellum, John Langellier, Alex Fejfar, and Olivia Garrison.

I would also like to thank Katy and Laine Morreau and the staff at Triumph Books for getting this book over the finish line.

To anyone I forgot or I did not have a chance to connect with, thank you as well.

# A Note on Sources

RECONSTRUCTING THE LIFE OF JACK TRICE WAS AN EXPANSIVE TASK that could not have been accomplished without the work of many who preceded me. There are two groups in particular without whose pioneering and invaluable work my book would not be possible. First and foremost are the archivists of Iowa State University's Jack Trice Papers, an essential collection of biographical material and news clippings about Trice, as well as photos and correspondence that once belonged to Trice himself, including his infamous "last letter." The second group comprises those whose writings on Jack have preserved his legacy, including Steven Jones (*Football's Fallen Hero*), Dorothy Schweider ("The Life and Legacy of Jack Trice"), Tom Emmerson ("Jack Trice"), and Jaime Schultz ("Stuff from which Legends Are Made"), among others.

The *Iowa State Daily* and *Ames Tribune* were foremost in providing context for a century-long span of life at ISU, and local newspapers including the *Cleveland Plain Dealer, Advocate, Seattle Times, Everett Herald, Kent Tribune, Ravenna Courier, Des Moines Register,* and *Cedar Rapids Gazette* were invaluable. Newspapers.com helped fill in additional blanks.

Ancestry.com and the Hiram County Historical Society held important details on Jack's family and early life.

Yearbooks for East Tech and Iowa State University were time capsules of different moments in Jack's timeline in life and death, and Everett High School's yearbook provided further information on Baggy's Boys.